The African-American Job Search

The African-American Job Search

Marc Sanders, M.A.

Writers Club Press
New York Lincoln Shanghai

Writers Club Press
an imprint of iUniverse, Inc.

For information address:
iUniverse
2021 Pine Lake Road, Suite 100
Lincoln, NE 68512
www.iuniverse.com

FIRST EDITION

ISBN: 0-595-26116-7

Printed in the United States of America

Contents

Foreword

"Success is not the result of spontaneous combustion...you must set your-self on fire."
—Reggie Leach, professional hockey player

The African-American Job Search was originally written to be a Web-based, distance learning course for online universities. When the course was originally conceived there were no books in libraries or bookstores that specifically targeted black job hunters. This omission not only deprives black job hunters of important race-specific employment information, but also adversely affects companies that miss hiring exceptional minority talent. There is a clear need for minority-focused job-finding resources.

Expansion of the course into a book meant supplementing original course materials and conducting additional research to ensure all the data is current. Special updates include the impact of September 11 on the job market, the latest Internet resources, an expanded section on employment discrimination laws and affirmative action (see Chapter 6), information about the thousands of newly-created government jobs, where the overseas jobs are, how to start a business and much more.

The primary goal of this book is to help you find employment using community resources, technology, the Internet (especially black-based Web sites in Chapter 3), and people within your social circles. The section on civil rights laws that protect minorities in the workplace will tell you what you can do if you believe discrimination has occurred. Can minorities use affirmative action to their advantage? You bet they can.

Increased attention on border protection and counterterrorism has created tens of thousands of new jobs with federal agencies like the Federal Bureau of Investigation (FBI), Central Intelligence Agency (CIA), and Immigration and Naturalization Service (INS). These organizations are in a hiring frenzy to fill positions of all kinds around the world. In fact, this employment sector is growing faster than almost any other. See Chapter 4 on how to apply for federal and other security-related jobs like those in airports.

Companies all across America are examining their minority recruitment practices and many have created "diversity departments" to address this important human resources function. You will learn which companies promote diversity and actively recruit minorities. Education and training are essential to staying competitive. Do you know how to get free training? I'll reveal secrets to getting free training in Chapter 4. Also covered are how to find the hottest new jobs, special tips for black women, and how to open previously-closed doors.

Writing an effective résumé and cover letter can help make a good first impression to a prospective employer. Does your résumé quickly convey to an employer how you would solve the employer's problem? How can key words ensure that your résumé is not discarded upon arrival? Chapter 5 will cover résumé and cover letter preparation. And when your knock-'em-dead résumé opens the door, you'll need to know how to conduct yourself in an interview. Chapter 8 will help you prepare for an outstanding interview.

Have you ever wanted to start your own business? In Chapter 7 get ideas for starting a small business and find out how other black entrepreneurs have fared. Do you know which American city is the best for a black American to start a business? What is a HUB and how can you take advantage of it? Have you heard about all the fun jobs on cruise ships and in national parks? How about finding a job through volunteering?

For answers and guidance to finding the perfect job, climb aboard and, as Reggie Leach suggests in the opening quotation, set yourself on fire. I'll show you how.

Acknowledgements

I would like to gratefully acknowledge the tremendous support of friends and family throughout this project. Special thanks to David Hemphill for his unwavering encouragement and providing delicious gourmet food and wine during particularly stressful times. I am also appreciative of the love and support of my mother, Ruthe, author of fifteen books about women's history, whose capable editorial skills resulted in a publishable manuscript. I also have the deepest affection and appreciation for my father, Tom, and my sisters, Martha, Debbie and Iwalani. My beloved cats, Syrus and Little Tiny One (all twenty-plus pounds of him) kept vigil while I labored at the computer.

Finally, the biggest reward in writing this book has been the terrific students who took the original Internet course and whose positive feedback has been so encouraging. The heartfelt messages I received from many intelligent black men and women about their job hunting experiences were quite a wake-up call about race in America. It is clear that the struggle for equal opportunity is far from over.

Introduction

The African-American Job Search will help minority job seekers find great jobs with organizations that are committed to workplace diversity. Whether you are a college graduate newly entering the job market, or a seasoned professional looking to change careers, you can benefit from this book. Not only will you learn how to create an outstanding résumé and cover letter, but also how to use minority-focused Web sites and understand employment bias and your legal rights. Remedies for incidents of race-based discrimination will be described in detail.

Following September 11, 2001, some changes occurred in the marketplace affecting several employment sectors. The impact of this event and its affect on job hunters will be thoroughly addressed.

In this book you will learn how to:

- Understand issues surrounding race in the workplace, what diversity means in corporate America today and, if black and female, what special challenges you face.
- Assess your skills and interests and develop a career plan.
- Utilize the Internet, especially black career Web sites, scan black periodicals to find jobs, and use ListServes, black college career services, and black professional and business associations.
- Research occupations and match them to your skills and personality.
- Prepare a professional résumé/cover letter and post on the Internet.
- Network, use the Minorities' Job Bank, find companies that have excellent minority hiring track records, and use affirmative action to your advantage.

- Explore job opportunities in non-profit organizations, with local, state and federal governments, on cruise ships, in the field of education, and more.
- Find jobs in the fields of security and counter-terrorism.
- Conduct yourself in an interview and negotiate salary.

To get the most benefits from this book and in your job search, it is suggested you have Internet access, a positive attitude, and perseverance. A college degree, specialized training or certifications, and foreign language skills are also excellent marketing tools.

For additional reading about some of the topics covered in this book, please see "Recommended Reading."

Chapter Summaries

Chapter 1—Does Race Still Matter?

Given that 22 percent of working blacks are still clustered in low-paying service and unskilled jobs, it appears racism is still endemic in the American workplace. This chapter will help you learn about the real world before you jump into the pool of job hunters. You will get the latest information about race in the workplace, what you should know as a black job hunter, the difference between affirmative action and diversity, how black women can succeed despite racism and sexism, and the best way to prepare yourself for a job in corporate America.

Chapter 2—Where Do You Want to Go?

This chapter will help you assess your current status and employment objectives and develop a long-range career plan that reflects your aptitudes and interests. Identifying your special talents will assist you in creating a personal marketing plan. You will also learn how your cultural background can be of value to an organization. Since most companies try to maintain good public images with respect to diversity, it has never been a better time to be a minority job seeker. A self-assessment exercise is included in this chapter.

Chapter 3—All About Black Resources

The World Wide Web is changing the way we search for jobs. Today there are dozens of outstanding Internet resources for African-American job hunters. This chapter will give you excellent tips for effectively using the Internet, from marketing yourself and joining a professional association, to finding the perfect black-friendly company. How to develop E-relationships to quickly exchange job information is covered, and you will learn how to use Web tools created for black job hunters and join black E-groups, ListServes, and chat rooms. I'll tell you how to find job leads by looking at black magazines. How can black elected officials assist you in your job search? Don't miss this chapter.

Chapter 4—Hot Jobs Today, Tomorrow and Beyond

This information-rich chapter will focus on current and future job trends. You will learn what types of jobs are in demand, what skills are needed to get them, and how to stay ahead of the career game. September 11th had a profound impact not only on the American psyche, but the economy and, consequently, the job market. Included in this chapter is the latest information about government and security jobs. How would you like to get free training? I'll tell you where to sign up. What organizations provide the training and opportunities necessary for you to succeed?

Chapter 5——Put it in Writing

Since a résumé is often your first contact with a prospective employer, it makes sense to do it right. You will learn how to compose attention-getting résumés and cover letters that highlight your skills and accomplishments. The various types of résumés will be described so you can create the one that best suits your background and qualifications. Résumé and cover letter samples are included. Then learn how to post them at the best black Web sites.

Chapter 6—Affirmative Action, Discrimination Laws, and Employment Agencies

This chapter will help minority job seekers take advantage of special opportunities to get hired, promoted, and advance their careers. Read about the Minorities' Job bank whose member companies are committed to workplace diversity. Affirmative action, a controversial policy, means different things to different people. Learn how affirmative action can be used to your advantage. You will find out what laws protect minority rights. Companies want to look good. They want you. How effective are employment agencies? Are they worth the fee? I'll tell you where to find job openings.

Chapter 7—Non-corporate, Overseas and Government Jobs

Non-profits not only perform community services they are also great places to learn new job skills. Find out if a non-profit is the right setting for you. Government jobs that offer outstanding benefits are growing rapidly for many reasons. There are hundreds of thousands of newly-created federal jobs in the wake of 9/11. For job seekers not into the typical 9-5, working on a cruise ship can offer non-traditional adventures. Perhaps you have always wanted to start a business. You'll read how to get free help from the experts. Have you ever considered owning a franchise? Would owning a KFC be aligned with your vision and goals? Minorities are being heavily recruited in all these areas. This chapter will also help you brainstorm new ideas for employment.

Chapter 8—"Tell Me About Yourself."

Although dreaded by many job hunters, the interview may be the most important part of getting a job. Not to worry. This chapter will give you several pointers in how to ace the interview. You will also learn how to research a company prior to the interview, how to stay positive during the process, and rehearse your answers for commonly asked questions. Nervous? I'll show you how to calm down when you get the jitters. After reading this chapter you should have the confidence to perform your absolute best. How and when should you negotiate salary? And if a job offer is extended at the interview, should you accept? Find out here.

CHAPTER 1

Does Race Still Matter?

"Prejudice is the child of ignorance."
—William Hazlitt (1780-1830), essayist, journalist

Racism is Alive and Well in the Workplace

Does equal opportunity exist today in America's job market? To a casual observer walking through corporate offices around the country, it might seem that it does not. It is rare today to see a person of color at the helm of a major corporation, and rarer still to see a woman of color in such a position. Yet there are many more doors open today to minorities, and opportunities are better now than at any other time. Diversity in the workplace is one of the most critical business issues facing organizations. Businesses are learning there are big payoffs to having workers from diverse backgrounds, including costs savings, having the best and the brightest in the country, the ability to compete in a wider variety of markets, and a public reputation for fairness. Organizations now know that cross-cultural teamwork and collaboration are essential to success. The truth is that differences are assets, rather than liabilities, since people of different backgrounds bring insights and bodies of knowledge that add value to organizations.

Black Role Models: Sanford and Son?

> *"A great many people think they are thinking when they are merely rearranging their prejudices."*
> —William James, 19th century psychologist

White Americans who don't personally know blacks get many of their images through entertainment and the mass media. Negative portrayals of black men as criminals, athletes, or corrupt politicians flood TV and the movies and these stereotypes shape people's opinions. Black male hip hop artists often receive extensive publicity because of aberrant or violent behaviors. These media stories help reinforce negative images of blacks. Incredible as it may seem, some white workers were recently polled about black men and the only positive trait they could describe was that they are good athletes!

There is a racial attitude continuum, and those with the least exposure to racial issues and diversity fall toward the high end of the racist scale. These attitudes certainly influence some of the people who make hiring decisions. People have traditionally hired others who most resemble themselves. You've probably heard the expression "Birds of a feather flock together." This also applies to the workplace. But times have changed—prejudice will no longer be tolerated in American companies.

Affirmative Action—Opening the Doors

> *"Ability is nothing without opportunity."*
> —Napoleon Bonaparte, French emperor

Affirmative action programs were originally designed to help qualified minorities receive employment in areas where they were once denied. But critics of affirmative action have argued for a long time that this policy constitutes reverse discrimination. However, when you think that just thirty years ago most jobs available to minorities were in low-skilled service and manufacturing and white males dominated professional jobs, it was time to make substantive changes. (No wonder they were called "white collar" jobs). Of course, at that time, many blacks lacked the academic qualifications for professional jobs. It was clear however, that something had to be done to broaden the range of opportunities for minorities and so affirmative action was born.

Isn't it really about opportunity? If doors to minorities are closed, then without breaking them down, how can blacks hope to achieve job equality with other Americans? Throughout this book you will learn ways to break through these barriers. Some of the most formidable tools to do this are a good education, the right attitude, knowledge of your legal rights, and the will to succeed.

What exactly is Affirmative Action?

Affirmative action, evolving out of policies designed to eradicate and overcome the effects of past discrimination in the United States, has three major goals: to overcome discrimination, increase diversity in the work force, and reduce poverty. The real push began with Presidents Kennedy, Johnson, and Nixon mandating "affirmative action" by federal contractors. The goal was to encourage the use of minority talent whenever possible. As these policies broadened, so did opposition to them. You will learn more about these policies and how they can help you in Chapter 6. (Source: Weiss, Robert, *We Want Jobs: A History of Affirmative Action*).

Why Haven't African-Americans Made Better Progress?

"Bigotry remains as entrenched and ubiquitous as ever."
—William Raspberry, Washington Post columnist (06/00)

Paycheck Parity

In 2000, for every dollar a white man earned a black man earned 76 cents. And the U.S. Bureau of Labor says that African-Americans were twice as likely to be unemployed as whites. In July 2001, the unemployment rate for all blacks hovered around eight percent—for black women it was six percent. (Source: U.S. Dept. of Labor). And the majority of blacks employed in good jobs still believe they have to be better performers than whites to get ahead. So, with all the efforts to promote equality and diversity in the workplace, why haven't African-Americans made better progress? One reason could be that many large corporations don't do anything concrete about promoting African-Americans until they receive negative publicity or lose a major discrimination lawsuit (Coca-Cola, after settling a $192 million racial-discrimination lawsuit in 2000, wants to ensure management is racially diverse. Minorities now make up 30% of its executive committee). But the real reason, as many people will readily admit, is that discrimination and prejudice still remain in the workplace. They are just more subtle.

Why, that's Reverse Discrimination!

A strident backlash against affirmative action began during the Reagan years. Conservative voices raised their opposition on talk shows and in newspaper columns. Corporations eventually shied away from discussing race and instead focused on workplace "diversity," to try to create a labor force that mirrors the population. To most Americans, the idea of diversity sounds more inclusive and less threatening than affirmative action. However, many African-Americans now feel the push for diversity has actually lessened opportunities for blacks because other minorities are now seeking the same jobs. There is competition for "affirmative action" jobs among Asians, women, blacks, Latinos, and the disabled. Legally protected groups are watching the pie shrink.

Black Women's Double Whammy

"The majority of the American people still believe that every single individual in this country is entitled to as much respect and dignity as every other individual."
—Barbara Jordan, former U.S. Congresswoman from Texas

Although faced with the double burden of racism and sexism, black women have made great progress in improving their economic status over the past decade. The goods news is that there are more black women than ever before in the workforce with many entering fields previously dominated by men. And the number of black women who own businesses is constantly rising. Despite these gains, black women, in general, earn less than similarly employed black men and experience higher unemployment than white women. According to the August 2001 report: "Highlight of Women's Earnings in 2000" by the U.S. Department of Labor, high school-educated white women's earnings ($500) were 16.6 percent higher than black women's ($429), and black women's earnings were 85.2 percent of black men's.

Education Pays

There is a direct connection between educational attainment and employment earnings. The more education a black woman has the higher her earnings and the less likely she will be unemployed. In 2000, women without a high school education earned $303 per week, compared with $760 for those with a college degree. (Source: U.S. Dept. of Labor, Report 952). Women working full time in professional occupations earned $725 per week. It would be accurate to claim that a college education pays off. It is important that black women prepare themselves for tomorrow's jobs by getting the necessary education, training and technical skills. Since women and minorities are one of the fastest growing segments of the labor force, businesses will be relying on these persons to satisfy their future labor needs.

"Broken spirits, unfulfilled dreams"

Black women actually hold more full-time jobs than white women. Eight out of every ten employed black women work full time, and part-time employment is also on the rise. (Source: U.S. Dept. of Labor). As companies try to control their labor costs by downsizing, many permanent full-time employees have been laid off and replaced with temporary, contract, or part-time workers. This type of work is known as *contingent work* and means anything other than the traditional eight-hour job. Whatever the type of work undertaken, women and minorities often have to put forth more effort and outperform their white counterparts to be considered equal among them. In spite of minorities and women's progress breaking through workplace barriers, a new type of discrimination is at work. This illegal artificial barrier, known as "the glass ceiling," is rooted in attitudinal or organizational bias and prevents minorities from advancing. According to Anthony Stith, author of *Breaking the Glass Ceiling: Sexism and Racism in Corporate America*, the glass ceiling "represents broken spirits, unfulfilled dreams, and loss of important contributions to our society."

Occupations for Black Women

Although traditional professions for black females have been primarily teaching and nursing, many have also moved into government service, sales, business, and office work. And more black women continue to enter higher-paying, career-oriented managerial and professional occupations that offer fringe benefits like health insurance, retirement plans, and paid vacations.

Eleven Leading Occupations for Employed Black Women in 2001
1. Nursing aides, orderlies, and attendants
2. Cashiers
3. Secretaries
4. Supervisors, personal service occupations
5. Retail sales (excluding cashiers)
6. Janitors and cleaners
7. Cooks
8. Maids
9. Registered nurses
10. Elementary school teachers
11. Social workers
[Source: U.S. Dept. of Labor Bureau Statistics]

In the next five years it is predicted that more than 10 million women will be in the labor force. Nontraditional service jobs such as police officers and firefighters that offer higher earnings than other service occupations continue to rapidly grow in popularity with women.

The number of businesses owned by black women at the turn of the 21st century rose to over 300,000. These black women-owned firms are excellent places for black women job hunters to find jobs and get mentoring. The Black Career Women's Web site at www.bcw.org also identifies and addresses the critical needs of black women in the workforce.

Color Blind? Not!

Despite the advances made by minorities, that pesky glass ceiling still exists in much of corporate white America. There are still few minority or women board members of the nation's Fortune 500 companies and fewer still in financial institutions. These injustices were addressed through affirmation action with mixed results. You will learn more about affirmative action's impact on your finding a job in a later chapter. But you should know that these programs have had a tremendous impact on economic growth for many minorities. It is still true however, that many whites feel unqualified minorities and women receive jobs at the expense of white males. Statistically, incidents of discrimination against minorities far outweigh complaints by a handful of disgruntled whites.

Diversity is In

Many corporations are doing everything they can to increase diversity. They did this at first because they didn't want to be sued for discrimination. But after having found great talent in the black community, they are going after it with gusto. In recent years several companies have added divisions to their human resources departments entirely devoted to achieving diversity objectives. These "diversity strategic planners" are installing organizational processes to address diversity and make the workplace comfortable for employees of all backgrounds.

The Workplace Diversity Network, a national association of community and business leaders, held a conference in 2001 in which a new mission statement was written that reflected a commitment to breaking down the barriers of racism. This statement, in part said that collectively as businesspeople, their mission is to, "Dismantle individual, cultural, and institutional racism by establishing and maintaining programs that increase multi-cultural awareness and cross-cultural competency, initiate collaborative relationships, promote mutual understanding and respect among all people, and develop inclusive organizations." Keep this groundbreaking statement by corporate America in mind as you look for a new job. Find out if the companies to which you apply hold membership in this association.

Black College Graduates—Create Your Future

"People don't plan to fail, they fail to plan."
—Anonymous

So you're finally graduating from college and ready to start your career. This is a very exciting time in your life and the decisions you make now may affect your career success. You gotta have a plan. Because if you don't have a plan for where you're going, you shouldn't be surprised by where you end up. A job is not just something you find in a newspaper ad—**a job is an opportunity to solve problems**—it is a way to challenge your skills and talents and express your values. The work world is filled with unlimited problems that need solutions. What type of interesting and challenging problems would you like to help solve? It's all about how you imagine your future. If you can picture yourself enjoying a fulfilling career, you can commit to creating it and begin to take action. The following chapters will help you bring about your vision and teach you to rely on ideas, people, resources, and opportunities to make it happen.

Your Mission...

Start with a personal career mission statement. To do this think about what is most important to you right now in the areas of work and career, personal and family, and self-improvement. There will be a brief exercise in the next chapter to help you evaluate your skills and accomplishments, but you should begin writing down your most satisfying accomplishments, whether they are job-related, family achievements, community work, hobbies, leisure activities, or things you accomplished in school. As your self-portrait evolves, you will get a better idea of what kind of job best suits your needs and temperament.

Attitude Adjustment

A national survey conducted in June 2000 by Rutgers University to assess workplace success rated traits such as a strong work ethic, integrity and sense of individual responsibility as being more important than computer or other occupational skills. Workplace success, according to the survey, is also dependent on critical thinking and communication skills. Of course, having the necessary skills to do the job is required, but making the transition from student to meaningful work means you must check your attitude. Employers are looking for candidates who have a positive attitude and can display this with enthusiasm. If you feel really good about yourself and are confident in your abilities, you will radiate an enthusiasm that is irresistible to employers.

Suggested Assignment: Compose a personal career mission statement to help you articulate your vision for building a career. Take an inventory of your experiences, skills, abilities, and accomplishments and include work and school experiences and any important personal activities. Based on where you've been, where do you want to go?

Young job seekers will find the book, *Job Power: The Young People's Job Finding Guide*, by Haldane, Bernard, and Jean, and Martin, Lowell to be helpful.

CHAPTER 2

Where Do You Want to Go?

Rev Your Engines

Have you thought about what motivates you? Is it just money or do you desire recognition in your field? Perhaps you would like to improve something or be in charge. When you engage in activities that best express your skills, you're more likely to feel good about yourself. This chapter will help you assess your current status and employment objectives and develop a long-range career plan that reflects your aptitudes and interests.

Develop Meaningful Personal Goals

To help you clarify your thoughts about work and personal life, answer these questions:

- What does success mean to me?
- How do my personal and work lives fit together?
- What am I willing to sacrifice to achieve success?

- What kind of rewards do I want once I'm successful?
- Is success worth what I have to do to get it?
- What keeps me from achieving my goals?
- Where do I see myself in five years? Ten years?

A Blueprint for Success

"It is never too late to be what you might have been."
—Mary Anne Evans, 19th century English novelist

Clarify what success means to you and how you can make it happen. Here is an outline to help you map your road to success:

- State your goals and objectives
- Develop a personal concept of success
- Identify productive and nonproductive habits
- Replace self-defeating habits with self-enhancing ones
- Overcome setbacks
- Make positive life choices that increase self-esteem
- To paraphrase the Army, be all that you are capable of
- Make the foregoing a habit

What's the difference between a job and a career? A job is a paycheck; a career is a future.

Getting to Know You

"We ask ourselves, who am I to be brilliant, gorgeous, talented and fabulous? Actually…who are you not to be?
—Nelson Mandela, human rights activist

If you are unsure about what you like to do and what you do well, then this process will help you to figure it out. Before you look for a job, you need to know what you're looking for. The better you know yourself and what you're good at, the better able you will be to envision suitable jobs and the more likely you'll find a job that matches your skills with interesting work.

The Self-Assessment Process

The three main steps to understanding yourself are:

a) Exploring your interests—Interests are things you like to do such as work with animals, use hand tools, sell, perform, help others with special needs and so on. Write down your three strongest interests.

b) Defining your skills and abilities—Skills and abilities can be grouped into categories like manual/physical, verbal, numerical (good with numbers), social, creative, administrative, care-giving, and investigative. What skills do you use when you are most happy? Write down three categories into which your skills might fit.

c) Clarifying your values—Identifying your values is an important part to this process. Values motivate you and can determine which jobs are right for you. If your job doesn't meet your needs or values, then expect to be disappointed. Values may include working alone or with others, helping improve the world, creativity, moral fulfillment, community, family, power and authority, financial gain, and stability, etc. Think of five values that best describe your needs. Which ones must be there for you to be happy in a job?

I Am Good At...

A skills inventory will help you determine your strengths, abilities, and how you handle problems, tasks and life experiences. Most skills fall into one of three categories: functional, adaptive, or specific. *Functional* skills deal with things, data or people, like accounting or teaching. *Adaptive* skills are personal traits like punctuality or getting along with people that can be adapted to a variety of settings. *Specific* skills are things like your typing speed, software proficiency, or ability to drive a school bus.

Do you like making things with your hands? Solving problems? What is your working style? Are you driven, patient, impulsive? Do you like multi-tasking or working on one task at a time? Do you want to make something (build a house) or offer a service? Perhaps you enjoy gathering or managing information. You might even like a combination of all three.

Accomplishments

> *"Every great personal victory was preceded by a personal goal or dream."*
> —Dennis Webb, success consultant

Accomplishments are not just experiences like winning a Nobel Prize, swimming the English Channel, or writing a best-selling novel, but anything you enjoyed doing that you did well and of which you were proud. This short survey will help you remember your accomplishments. Why is this important? Because when we accomplish something, we feel valuable and our self-esteem rises.

- What are some of your main accomplishments?
- What did you enjoy the most when doing them?
- What did you do the best?
- What was your motivation?
- How did you get started?
- Did you work alone or with others?
- In what kind of environment was this done?

The Key to Success

To become successful you need to create a lifestyle that is true to who you are and what you want to achieve.

Choreography to getting results:

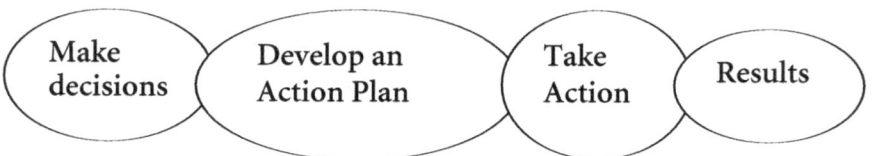

Where Do I Fit In?

"The man who is born with a talent which he has meant to use finds his greatest happiness in using it."
—Johann Wolfgang Goethe, playwright and poet

What combination of abilities and talents make you right for a specific job? Now that you have a clearer picture of your skills and accomplishments, what careers might suit you? We'll be exploring hot new careers in a later chapter, but it doesn't hurt to start thinking about a possible industry you might enjoy working in. Career choices are influenced by these factors:

- the population you wish to serve
- the work environment you prefer
- the kind of people you work with
- your long-term goals
- your values
- the job market
- location
- the requirements for the job

The Scene

Understanding the type of work environment in which you thrive will help you achieve success. Some people prefer a relaxed, laid back office while others like more structure. A creative person might not be happy as a bank teller whereas someone with conservative values might enjoy an office with a more formal atmosphere and where roles are clearly defined. To learn about a corporation's environment get a copy of the company's annual report, its newsletter, check its Web site, visit the office, ask someone in human resources, and learn about its mission, etc. Rate these common work quality issues on a scale from 1 to 10 to help you clarify the type of organization where you would be happiest.

- Working with people I like
- Accomplishing important things
- Becoming competent in my field
- Having quality time with family
- Helping people
- Doing challenging work
- Being recognized as a leader
- Being able to live where I want
- Having authority over others

If you rated leadership as important, then you will want to look at organizations that offer advancement and leadership opportunities.

Where do you want to be in five years?

> *"Afoot and light-hearted*
> *I take to the open road,*
> *Healthy, free, the world before me,*
> *The long brown path before me,*
> *Leading where I choose."*
> —Walt Whitman, poet

Since you determine your own success, your goals must be clearly stated so you know what you must do to accomplish them. There are both short-term and long-term goals to consider.

Do you think carefully about what you want and then go after it with total commitment? Most of us either wish things would happen to us (like win the lottery) or we write our secret life wishes in a journal, but we don't have a map of how to get there. Is your goal believable? If you don't believe in your own talents, then how can you have your dream career?

If you are a recent college graduate, then your goal chart will look different than a seasoned worker's. For the former, your immediate goal may be to find a job as soon as possible. You will probably want to create and post your résumé at several online databases and maybe to some electronic recruiters. (See Chapter 5). Whatever your situation is, the first step is to know yourself. Next, you will want to learn what's out there. Networking should be an ongoing activity no matter what your employment status (more on how to network later). When you identify a job opportunity that sounds promising, ask yourself how it will fit into your long-term career goals. Perhaps you've always wanted to go back to college and finish your degree, or learn HTML. Those are measurable goals. To ensure your goals are meaningful, make them "SMART:"

-   Specific
-   Measurable
-   Action-oriented
-   Realistic
-   Time-based.

Five steps to goal setting

1. Focus your thinking
2. Create a plan
3. Develop and maintain a burning desire
4. Build supreme confidence
5. Work with total commitment.

Social Security Required

Whatever your background, skills or experience, no legitimate organization will hire you without a Social Security number. The Social Security federal program was established in the 1930s to assist American wage-earners by providing a retirement account in their senior years. A percentage of wages is deducted from each paycheck and invested in a personal retirement account. If you already have a Social Security number and want more information and access to your account, visit the Social Security Administration's Web page, "The Official Website of the Social Security Administration." There is even a career link for persons interested in employment with this agency. (Source: www.ssa.gov).

If you have not applied for a Social Security number and card you will need to complete Form SS-5 (available for download at www.gov/online/ss-5.html), obtain one by calling 1-800-772-1213, or visit your local Social Security office. Do not make up a fraudulent Social Security number as companies use software to detect bogus numbers.

With your application for a Social Security number you will need to submit at least two documents as evidence of your age, identity, and U.S. citizenship or lawful alien status. Acceptable identity documents are:

- driver's license
- marriage or divorce records
- military records
- employer ID card
- adoption record
- life insurance policy
- passport
- health insurance card (not Medicare card)
- school ID card

If you have been granted alien status and want a Social Security card you must produce unexpired documents issued to you by the U.S. Immigration and Naturalization Service (INS), such as Form I-551, I-94, I688B, or I-766. If you are here lawfully, a Social Security card will be issued to you. (Source: www.ssa.gov).

Get Ready to Launch

"We make our own fortunes and we call them fate."
—Disraeli, 19th century British Chancellor

Marketing

Think about how to market yourself. Try to do something every day that moves you closer to your goal of getting a job. Marketing is basically displaying yourself and talents to interested buyers. You are going to use the latest technology to market yourself in multiple locations, but more about this later.

Some marketing tools you will be using include research, phone calls, the Internet, snail mail, e-mail, faxing, and socializing. You will get some scripts for making effective phone calls in a future chapter.

Remember, to get hired you have to decide what you want to get across, do it convincingly, and lead the buyer to ask, "Can I use this person, and for what?" You must be very clear about what you do.

Elevator Speech

An elevator speech is a brief description of something about yourself you can convey to someone else in the time it takes to ride an elevator. Write a paragraph describing what you do and memorize it so when you run into people who can contribute to your success, you can tell them. Be clear.

Examples of Unclear and Clear:
1. Unclear: I'm into computers.
   Clear: I manage payroll databases.
2. Unclear: I am really good around the office.
   Clear: I type 70 words per minute and know Microsoft Office.

The Networking List

Start a list of all the people you know including family, friends, doctors, and neighbors, etc. Keep adding names as you remember them. You'll be using this list later.

In job hunting, networking is a way of building relationships with those who may have access to leads, either directly or indirectly, that may lead to a job. This does not mean approaching strangers and thrusting your résumé in their face. Rather, creative and productive networking reaps dividends. The first thing to do is start with a need, followed by identification of others who share the same needs, resulting in a contact or relationship.

Need (goal) + Identification of others = Contact

Good networkers are information gatherers and adept at socializing. The next time you are at a professional meeting or conference, watch how the networking pros work the room. They are usually masterful communicators and at ease with people of all backgrounds.

Black entrepreneur and author Earl Graves says in his book, *How to Succeed in Business without Being White,* there is a terrific black business network in the U.S. that "is an incredibly vital aspect of the African-American community—and one of our best tools for competing in the white-dominated business world." So start thinking about ways to plug into this black business network. The next chapter offers tips for building your network.

Tip: To become a good networker, become a better listener by being attentive, focusing on the speaker, and showing interest in what he or she is saying.

Good Habits

"The only difference between those who have failed and those who have succeeded lies in the difference of their habits. Good habits are the key to all success. Bad habits are the unlocked door to failure."
—Og Mandino, Inspirational Author

Without developing good habits, like reviewing your to-do list every day, making phone calls and checking e-mail, etc., you will make little if any progress.

You are the architect of your own life.

CHAPTER 3

All about Black Resources

Tell-a-Friend, Tele-phone, Tell-the-Net

"You must develop a contact network. It is the most essential, most effective, and least expensive marketing technique available and you cannot succeed without it."
—Jeffrey Lant, marketing guru

People may well be your most important resource. Look closely at successful men and women…one thing they have in common is they've become successful through the help of people in their network. People can provide leads, refer contacts, and hire you. *A lead is knowledge of an opportunity that may lead to a job.* The more people you include in your network, the more potential leads you will have.

Try not to feel like you're using people when you ask for assistance. Rather, frame your request in a way that reveals your admiration for their expertise. Example: "Mr. Jones, since you have a reputation in your field for being the best, I'll bet you know the answer to my question," or "know to whom I should speak about a job." Most people are flattered when asked to share their wisdom or exercise their influence.

Getting the Leads

In Chapter 2 it was suggested you begin making a list of everyone you know so you can find out as much as possible about the job market. Don't overlook the importance of family. You would be surprised at how many people they know.

People Who Need People

People in your personal and professional circles comprise your network and can furnish you job leads. Your network can be drawn from people on this list.

Your Family	**Friends**
Siblings, aunts, uncles, cousins	Neighbors
Spouse/significant other	Spouse's friends
In-laws	Parents of your children's friends
Exes and ex in-laws	Social organizations (bridge club...)
Personal	**Professional**
Clergy	Doctor, dentist, etc.
PTA members	Accountant, stockbroker
Fraternity/sorority members	Banker
Former classmates	Insurance agent
Former teachers	Realtor
Former co-workers	Plumber, carpenter, etc.
	Barber/hairdresser

Work the Network

To be successful in networking you need to know what you are selling (you) and who the buyers are (your job target). Make at least five calls every day to different people in your network. The purpose of these calls is to inform your network of your career plans and to solicit their help in finding you a job. Start a networking diary to keep track of everyone you talk to, and separate the hot from the lukewarm leads. Essentially, you're looking for buyers to tell about yourself.

What to Say

Call a friend/associate (A) and explain that you are looking for a job and ask if he/she knows about any openings in your field.

A suggests you call B, who may have an opening or knows someone who does. You contact B and explain that A suggested you call. (A is the bridge in your network).

B explains that he/she has no openings but suggests you call C. Since you don't really know B, however, this may feel uncomfortable. But C is still a potential source of important information, so pursue the contact. The more people you know and who know you, the greater your chances of finding a terrific job opening.

Tip: If you have trouble getting someone by phone during normal business hours, try again between 6:00 p.m. and 7:00 p.m. This has been shown to be the best time to reach many people.

Don't be shy. Strike up conversations with people you meet on a plane or at a party and let them know you're job hunting. Deliver your elevator speech. Start a networking log to help you keep track of every-one you meet. Be sure and highlight the hot leads for future reference. Your log might look something like this:

Networking Log

Names & Organizations	Objectives	Results
Johnny Walker ABC Software, Inc.	To arrange lunch meeting to talk about job openings	Lunch – May 16th, 12:00 Bring résumé – Hot
Big City Corporation 5678 Main St.	To meet HR director at the annual meeting	Calendared – Warm

Another way to network is to write letters to former colleagues, dis-tant relatives and acquaintances. This is called a *networking letter* and in it you will tell your reader about your job search, what you want to have happen in the future (in terms of reaching your career goals), and how they can help you reach those goals. The general purpose is to get people who can help you to do so.

Sample Networking Letter
Dear (Contact's name),

I came across your name in my address book and remembered how much fun we had at that seminar in Las Vegas last year (small talk in this paragraph). Congratulations on the (birth of your new baby, promotion, anniversary, etc.).

I just wanted to drop you a note to let you know how I am doing. I've recently decided to make a career change and am very excited about my future. My (# of years) experience in (fill in your know-how here) has expanded my career possibilities, and I'm confident that any worthwhile company would hire me in a second if they knew what I could offer.

You've always known so many people. Can I send my résumé to you in a few days to look over? I would welcome your suggestions. Feel free to pass on my résumé to your friends in case they know of any job openings. I am willing to relocate, depending on the circumstances.

I hope to see you at the Smith's Christmas party in December.

Your Friend,

Your Name

Black Elected Officials

Some of the most powerful and respected people in the black community are its elected public officials. Articulate and hardworking, most of these men and women haven't forgotten their roots and are still strongly connected to their communities. They are often delighted to help their constituents and sometimes a simple phone call and request for assistance are all it takes.

Today you will find black elected officials in all areas of public life. At the local level there are black city council members, city supervisors, aldermen and alderwomen, county commissioners, judges and school board members. At the state and national levels are legislative bodies consisting of African-American senators and representatives. These folks can be found in the Blue Pages section of the telephone directory or in your state's legislative directory. If you don't know who your representatives are, call your public library and ask the information desk which of them is African-American. Remember, they are called public servants for a reason.

Sample Phone Call to Elected Official

In a 90-second script try to establish who you are and why you are calling. Your conversation might go something like this.

(The receptionist answers).

"Hello, my name is (your name). I live in Senator/Representative (his or her name's) district and I'd like to speak to him/her. It's a personal matter and won't take very much time." (Keep trying to get the party on the line even if you have to leave messages in earlier attempts).

(Elected official picks up). "Hello Senator/Representative _____, how are you today? I know you're very busy so I won't take up much of your time. I'm calling because I am between jobs, and given your reputation in the black community for getting things done, I thought you would be the perfect person to speak to.

I want to use my talents to make a real difference and I know there's a perfect job out there for me. I was hoping you would know someone who might need a skilled, hard-working black man/woman like myself. An opening at a minority-owned company would be ideal, but I thrive in many kinds of environments. Anyway, I'm very good at _____ and _____ and enjoy (working with people, making things, etc., whatever you do well).

If you have a few minutes to meet with me in person, I would be most appreciative. Oh, next Wednesday at 2:00? That would be perfect! I'll bring my résumé. I'm looking forward to meeting you. Thank you very much for your time today. Goodbye."

It Could Happen!

If you happen to snare an invitation to meet with an important contact, make a good impression and act professionally so that person becomes interested in you within the first few minutes. Practice saying who you are, what special thing you have to offer, what you're looking for, and what you would like the contact to do for you. Make the request concrete. For example, would you like them to make a phone call? Write a reference?

Black Organizations

More black organizations exist today than ever before. There is likely at least one group that meets your individual needs and tastes. You can find a lot of information about these organizations in libraries and on the Internet. Many of these organizations' missions include helping blacks find employment. The black-focused organizations listed below may be helpful in finding a job.

NAACP	National Urban League	National Urban League
Attn: Programs Dept.	Career Center	Washington Operations
4805 Mount Hope Dr.	120 Wall Street	1111 14th St., NW
Baltimore, MD 21215	New York, NY 10005	Suite 1001
(410) 358-8900	(212) 558-5300	Washington, D.C. 20005
www.naacp.org	www.nul.org	(202) 898-1604

Note: The NAACP's Programs Department holds annual regional and national career fairs. Contact your regional NAACP office to get career fair dates (or visit their Web site at www.naacpjobfair.com) for information about local companies that have a good record for hiring minorities.

Other black organizations include the Southern Christian Leadership Conference, the National Association of Colored Women's Clubs, the YMCA and YWCA, the National Council of Negro Women, black chambers of commerce (usually in large cities), black churches, trade unions, and black professional associations (accountants, dentists, engineers, etc.). These Web sites will be listed later. Black colleges often have career placement services that help you every step of the way.

To find black associations in your area, check the Yellow Pages or go to this Web site: www.ntu.edu.sg/home/ctng/assoc.htm.

Chambers of Commerce

Chambers of commerce can be found in many cities and are excellent resources for job hunters and networking. Most chambers' missions are more than just providing resources for business owners; they are also interested in publicizing, promoting, and developing commercial and industrial opportunities in their areas. Many chambers take an active role in improving schools, streets, housing, public works, fire and police protection, parks, and playgrounds. Members consist of businesses of all types and sizes that pay membership dues and are eligible for a variety of benefits, discounts, resources, and networking opportunities. Find your local chamber of commerce phone number and call them to request more information about member companies. With this information you can get the names of the decision-makers in each company. A chamber of commerce is also a good place to find a mentor and learn leadership skills. Many chambers have special programs designed to groom promising young persons to become the next generation of leaders. There are also several black chambers of commerce in many cities. Check to see if there is one in your town. They'd love to hear from you.

The E-Generation

The World Wide Web is changing the way we search for jobs. The old method of sending one résumé at a time to someone who might not be interested is obsolete. With Internet technology you can be "seen" in hundreds of markets by thousands of prospective employers. According to the Wall Street Journal 80% of all recruiters spend time online searching for potential candidates. And using the Net can help you target your efforts more efficiently.

Have you already joined the electronic generation? If you haven't had an opportunity to "surf the Web," then I strongly suggest you find a computer with an Internet connection and get plugged in. Your job search will be that much easier if you are familiar with the Internet. Public libraries, cyber-cafes, airports, universities, community centers and job training centers often have Internet connections. The Internet has become an indispensable tool to millions of people. Don't let the Digital Divide (the economically-based gap between those with and without computers and Internet access) deprive you of deserved opportunities. The book, *Job Searching Online for Dummies*, by Pam Dixon, is an excellent resource to help job hunters tap into the World Wide Web.

Black Web Sites

African-American Web sites are terrific places to discover what's happening in black communities everywhere. You can also join a chat room, check job information, read movie reviews, get discounts on products and services and weather forecasts for any location, shop, apply for credit and much more. When visiting these sites as a job hunter, your goal is to get ideas and leads for jobs.

The sheer volume of Web sites can be somewhat overwhelming causing information overload, not to mention the seemingly endless links. However, surfing the Web will pay off in the long run. To get specific information (what Pam Dixon calls "link-mining" in her book about job searching online) about a company, go to the site's home page and scan it. A good company's Web site has information that includes:

- A search feature
- A contact link
- An employment link
- A company information link
- A product/service link
- A list of recent customers

Some company sites include biographical sketches and photos of corporate honchos. Learn about the corporate mission; check out the customer list to gauge the stature of the company; then go to the employment page and e-mail a letter or scannable résumé (more on that in Chapter 5) to the person who makes hiring decisions.

To find region-specific job information go to www.yahoo.com and type the name of the city that interests you. Another site where you can investigate jobs in specific geographic areas is www.citysearch.com.

Black and Diversity-focused Web Sites

Check out the following outstanding black-focused Web Sites and bookmark your favorite ones. After you write your résumé (in Chapter 5) you will want to post it at some of the sites that appeal to you.

www.bdpa.org—Black Data Processor Associates; links to local chapters

www.BlackEnterprise.com—"The virtual desktop for African-Americans"

www.blackeoejournal.com—Black Equal Opportunity Employment Journal Magazine; "Keeps America in touch with all minorities by providing career opportunities, community awareness, and higher education."

www.BlackWeb.net—news, culture, networking, and employment

www.BlackVoices.com—780,000 members and a career center

www.Blinks.net—technology-oriented with a career center

www.DiversityCareers.com—careers in engineering and information technology

www.DiversityInc.com—career center and excellent minority resources www.DiversityEmployment.com—a multicultural employment site offering a job and résumé database

www.Diversitylink.com/index.htm—a virtual community of diversity professionals

www.diversityrecruiting.com/index2.html—introducing diversity candidates to America's best companies to work for in professional, technical and managerial positions

www.diversitysearch.com/index2.html—a woman-owned site, "helping to promote diversity in the workplace"

www.eop.com—Equal Opportunity Publications, Inc.; "Leaders of Diversity Recruitment for over 30 Years"

www.EverythingBlack.com—business, culture, education, etc.

www.HireDiversity.com—employment resources for minorities

www.IMDiversity.com—search jobs, post résumés, check employer profiles

www.LittleAfrica.com—marketplace, communities, careers, resources

www.minority-professionalnetwork.com—choose desired metropolitan area

www.netnoir.com—the black network

www.nsbe.org/—National Society of Black Engineers

www.ReadingBlack.com—literary news, calendar of events, and jobs section

www.TBWT.com—The Black World Today; offers free résumé hosting

The Minorities' Job Bank

One of the best Web resources for black job hunters is the Minorities' Job Bank (www.iminorities.com). Sponsored by the *Black Collegian* magazine (see below), this site provides excellent career information for entry-level job hunters and skilled professionals. Many different ethnic groups are linked to this site. After registering, you can create a "job seeker" account that lets you

- build/store your résumé
- search for the latest job postings
- have a search agent notify you by e-mail when a job listing matches your criteria
- read the latest news affecting minority job hunters.

The "Career Development" page offers articles and tips on minority workplace issues, job search strategies, résumé writing, interviewing techniques, networking, affirmative action, and even tips for relocating. Don't miss this one.

Some company members of this job bank are America Online, America West Airlines, Bank of America, Best Buy, Coors Brewing Company, Eli Lilly and Company, Cisco Systems, Sprint Corporation, and K-mart.

African-American Periodicals

Here are some of the more popular black periodicals. (A comprehensive list of African-American publications can be found at www.aawc.com/aap.html).

www.Ebony.com
www.Essence.com
www.Jet.com
www.Black-Collegian.com—outstanding career site for students of color; sponsors the Minorities' Job Bank

Tip: Look at black magazine advertisements to see which companies market to the black community. They probably have friendly hiring policies toward blacks and are therefore excellent prospects for job leads.

ListServes

ListServes are public or private groups of people with similar interests who communicate through e-mail. Easy to join, they are tremendously useful for networking. As of this writing there are over 100,000 lists concerning every topic imaginable. After you find a list you like, subscribe to it, post your own messages and read others' messages. You'll be able to exchange mail, join chat rooms, and stay abreast of what's happening in your virtual community. These are great for announcing new job openings before anyone else hears about them. One of the more popular sites for creating groups is www.groups.yahoo.com.

E-mail

If you do not already have an e-mail account that enables you to send and receive e-mail then you are depriving yourself of an indispensable resource. There are several Internet Service Providers (ISPs) and Web sites that allow you to set up a free e-mail account, albeit with restrictions. These include Yahoo, MSN Hotmail (one of the largest), and Terra Lycos. Create an e-mail account today.

Search Engines

Search engines are like Web librarians that help you find something in the Web "card catalog." Some engines do a broad search while others narrow the search to a specific database. The clearer your search request, the better "hits" will appear. Hits are links that might be related to the information you are seeking.

To use a search engine, go to the Web site and type in your keyword or question. At sites like Ask Jeeves (www.ask.com) you can ask your question in plain English like, "Where can a minority find a construction job in California?" Try not to be overwhelmed by the volume of information. Often you can get your answer the first or second try. But if you have time, it's fun to explore search engines to see how far they will take you.

Some of the more popular search engines are:

AltaVista	www.altavista.com
Ask Jeeves	www.ask.com
Complete Planet (over 103,000 databases)	www.completeplanet.com/
Expert Central	www.expertcentral.com

Google	www.google.com
Hotbot (Terra Lycos network)	www.hotbot.com
Invisible Web	www.invisibleweb.com/
MetaCrawler	www.metacrawler.com
New York Times	www.nytimes.com/library/tech/reference/cynavi.html
Web Data	www.webdata.com/

Tip: Bookmark your favorite Web sites so you don't have to type in the address each time.

The Top Job Databases on the World Wide Web

Tens of thousands of employers post job openings on hundreds of employment sites every day. The following sites contain the largest number of positions with the most active online résumé databases. At these sites you can search for jobs by field/industry, geographic location, and salary, and post your résumé.

All Retail Jobs—largest recruiter of retail jobs	www.allretailjobs.com
America's Job Bank—over one million jobs by zip codes	www.ajb.dni.us
Best Jobs USA—extensive career site	www.bestjobsusa.com
Brass Ring—technology-heavy	www.brassring.com
Career Babe—career division for online job searches	www.careerbabe.com
Career Builder—over 400,000 jobs	www.careerbuilder.com
Career Center—general site for jobs here and abroad	www.careercenter.net
Career City—a very nice site; has "Diversity Job Center"	www.careercity.com
Career Journal—Wall Street Journal's site	www.careerjournal.com
Career Mosaic—mostly technical/financial	www.careermosaic.com
Career Path—find jobs by industries	www.careerpath.com

Career Shop—post résumés, get career advice, training	www.careershop.com
Career Tips—interesting site on careers around the world	www.careertips.com
Employment Guide—outstanding site	www.employmentguide.com
Employment Spot—outstanding clearinghouse	www.employmentspot.com
Flip Dog—370,810 jobs by location/category	www.flipdog.com
Headhunter.net	www.Headhunter.net
Hire.com	www.hire.com
Hot Jobs	www.hotjobs.com
Hot Résumés—post yours here	www.hotresumes.com
JobOptions.com—joined with FlipDog	www.joboptions.com
High tech career site	www.hightechcareers.com
Job.com	www.job.com
Jobs Online	www.jobsonline.com
Jobs.com	www.jobs.com
Kaplan Careers	www.kaplancareers.com
Monster.com—among the largest	www.monster.com
Riley Guide—gateway job site, employment resources	www.rileyguide.com
Wet Feet—company info, industry profiles	www.wetfeet.com
Workzone.net	www.workzone.net

What Jobs Are Advertised Online?

Some of the most commonly advertised jobs advertised on the Internet are technical, engineering, sales and marketing, administrative, telecommunications, communications/public relations, financial services, teaching, medical, legal and business/professional services. The hottest new jobs on the market today will be covered in the next chapter.

If you are a recent college graduate, check out these sites for help finding a job:

www.asktheheadhunter.com—fun, hip and entertaining
www.campuscareercenter.com—college grad focus
www.collegegrad.com—a comprehensive entry-level job site
www.jobtrak.com—part of Monster.com
www.truecareers.com—search jobs; create a résumé

Chat Resources

If you have a Web browser like Internet Explorer or Netscape Communicator you can visit chat rooms and start chatting. A chat room allows you send messages to a group of people in real (synchronous) time, meaning you don't have to wait for an e-mail response. Just type a message and transmit it immediately to an area where other chatters see it and can respond. Chat rooms are a terrific way to network and find experts in your particular industry. To find experts chatting online, go to www.talkcity.com and type in your user name. Click on the Go Chat button or on one of the topics that interest you. To access a chat on the list, click on the highlighted link and follow directions. According to the Wall Street Journal there are 1.4 million active chat rooms on any given day. Although some chat rooms have topics that are juvenile or offensive, the following chat sites are considered superior:

www.cnn.com
www.msnbc.com
www.chatlist.com

Note: Web addresses change periodically, so don't be discouraged if you can't find a particular site. There are more than enough cyberspace resources out there, even if the site you are searching for has vanished into virtual oblivion.

Black-Friendly Companies

America is starting to wake up and smell the "diversity-is-hip" coffee. There are numerous benefits to hiring minorities, particularly their experiences and ideas that ultimately enhance a company's competitive edge. Organizations that embrace minorities also enjoy not only expanded customer bases but good public relations.

The Best Companies for Minorities

According to Fortune Magazine the following ten companies are rated as being the best for blacks in areas such as percentage of black managers, philanthropy to black communities, cultural sensitivity, and training, etc.:

Fannie Mae—www.fanniemae.com; CEO is Franklin Raines, a black man

DTE Energy—www.dteenergy.com; uses lots of minority-owned vendors

United Parcel Service—www.ups.com; more than half of all new hires are minorities

BellSouth—www.bellsouthcorp.com

U.S. Postal Service—www.usps.com

Coca-Cola—www.cocacola.com

McDonald's—www.mcdonalds.com

Advantica—www.advantica-dine.com—owns Denny's restaurants

The New York Times Company—www.nytco.com

FedEx—www.fedex.com

A complete list of the 50 best companies for minorities can be found at www.fortune.com/lists/diversity/index.html.

(Source: http://www.fortune.com/lists/diversity/minority_group.html).

It's the "Real Thing"

The Coca-Cola Corporation, defendant in two highly public employment bias lawsuits in the late 1990s, is now a good company for blacks to get an executive job because of past unfavorable publicity and its desire to be a good corporate citizen. There has never been a better time than now to be black and job hunting.

Minority-owned businesses

To get a list of minority-owned businesses check with the U.S. Census Bureau's Company Statistics Division. Data from extensive surveys is published as part of an economic census and these reports are available to the public. Researching a company can help you find job openings, learn about a particular industry, prepare for an interview, and negotiate salary. Look for information such as products and services, competitors, types of customers, location, rank in the industry, sales and profit trends, and strategic plans.

Tip: To get detailed company information online, visit: http://business.lycos.com/companyresearch/crtop.asp

CHAPTER 4

Hot Jobs Today,
Tomorrow and Beyond

*"We should all be concerned about the future because we will have to
spend the rest of our lives there."*
—Charles Kettering, inventor with General Motors Corp.

In this chapter find what jobs are currently in demand and learn
about the new ones being created by the technology economy and post
9/11 security concerns. Employers, both private and public, are looking
for people with all kinds of skills for these jobs. With the wartime economy shifting into high gear, the federal government has created tens of
thousands of new jobs to fill several industries where there is demand.
The savvy job hunter knows not only where to look for openings, but
also what types of jobs are out there. The better prepared you are the
easier it will be to find unpublished jobs and information about your
preferred industry.

The Future's So Bright...Just Take off the Shades

In a previous chapter you completed a self assessment profile and,
hopefully, learned some important things about yourself, like your

strengths, values and accomplishments. You can't easily convince an employer that you're right for a job if you don't know who you are. A job that is aligned with your values and preferences is more likely to "take." To help you sort through your thoughts you can create a short personal checklist to help you match careers to your specific requirements. Just because everyone you know is learning Web page design or selling real estate doesn't mean those are the right careers for you. People who like social settings wouldn't enjoy sitting in front of a computer all day without human interaction. You will know in your heart if a situation is right for you.

The Only Sure Thing is Change

A decade ago few, if any of you, heard of the Internet. You probably didn't use e-mail, didn't know what a Web manager did, and thought faxes were cool. Cell phones didn't fit into people's pockets and mapping the human genome was science fiction. Well, readers, the future has arrived. Things change very quickly, and our work and world are permanently affected. Forget about getting jobs the old way. It's a whole new world. If you have the knowledge, then you got the power.

New Trends

According to a *Time Magazine* cover story (spring 2000), 90% of all white-collar jobs in the United States will be gone or altered in the next decade. Even business functions like personnel, sales, accounting, production, and vendor relationships, etc., will quickly change as new software continues to be developed. Say goodbye to professional paper pushing and hello to white-collar robots. The other ongoing trend is more people telecommuting, i.e., working at home, but connected to the workplace via modem, fax and phone.

In Olden Days…

In the old days you worked for a paycheck, got a Christmas bonus, retired after forty years, and that was it. Back then if you worked hard and were loyal, you were sometimes guaranteed a job for life. Today the "contract" between employer and employee has changed. Workers demand comfortable and ergonomically correct work environments, fringe benefits like health care and retirement, stock options, family-friendly policies, and input into how organizations are managed. Employees are there *voluntarily* because many can leave at will and (hopefully) get a better gig. This doesn't mean, however, that employers don't still have stringent requirements for employees.

New Technology = Change

Changing technology means there are more career opportunities than ever before, especially in information services, medical technology, communications, computers, engineering and home-based businesses. All of these fantastic new jobs are wide open but there's a lot of competition for them. If you notice an opportunity and hesitate, someone else will snatch the job you've been eyeing. Of course, if you jump on something and it later turns out to not be a good match, you may simply withdraw your application.

Fastest-Growing Occupations

According to the U.S. Department of Labor's Bureau of Labor Statistics, these jobs will continue to grow at a rapid clip through 2005. [* = requires college degree]

1. Home health aides
2. Systems analysts/computer scientists *
3. Physical therapists *
4. Medical assistants
5. Security professionals
6. Human service workers
7. Radiology technicians
8. Medical secretaries

9. Physical therapy aides
10. Psychologists *
11. Correction officers
12. Data processing equipment repairers
13. Flight attendants
14. Computer programmers *
15. Occupational therapists *
16. Surgical technologists
17. Medical records technicians
18. Management analysts *
19. Respiratory therapists
20. Childcare workers
21. Marketing/advertising/public relations managers *
22. Legal secretaries
23. Receptionists
24. Registered nurses *
25. Nursing aides/orderlies
26. Cooks, restaurant workers
27. Teachers *
28. Social Workers *
29. Podiatrists *
30. Lawyers *

The Government Printing Office sells publications on the outlook for different occupations. These publications can be ordered through The Bureau of Labor Statistics Publication Sales Center, P.O. Box 2145, Chicago, IL 60690, (312) 353-1880. Call or write for titles and prices. Payment by check, money order, VISA, MasterCard or GPO deposit account must accompany your order. Make your check or money order payable to the Superintendent of Documents.

Here are projected trends for the following occupational areas:

Occupational Group	Trends
Executive, administrative and managerial	Hot
Professional specialties (architects, lawyers…)	Hot
Technicians and support occupations	Very Hot
Marketing and Sales	Lukewarm
Administrative Support/Clerical	Cold
Service occupations	Hot
Security	Very Hot
Agriculture, Forestry, Fishing, etc.	Lukewarm
Mechanics and Repairers	Warm
Construction	Warm
Transportation and Material Moving	Hot
Laborers and helpers	Warm

For more information on job trends, read *The Unofficial Guide to Hot Careers*, by Shelly Field, ISBN: 0-02-863416-0.

Time Magazine's List of the Hottest Jobs in the Next 10 Years

These jobs sound like they belong in a science-fiction movie.

- Tissue engineers (grow new skin, organs, and body replacement parts)
- Gene programmers (genetically modify bio-organisms)
- Pharmers (crop and animal genetic engineering)
- Frankenfood monitors (people who check effects of genetic manipulation of food)
- Data miners (research experts/information gatherers)
- Hot-line handymen (home electronics diagnosticians)
- Virtual reality actors (and scriptwriters for cyberspace dramas)
- Narrowcasters (personalized broadcasting for your particular tastes and shopping habits)

- Turing testers (people who make computers more human-like)
- Knowledge engineers (artificial intelligence brokers that translate your expertise into software)

UPDATE: Since the Hot Jobs section was originally written, September 11, 2001 somewhat altered the jobs landscape. As many businesses failed during the fallout of that catastrophic event, other ripples were felt throughout the labor market. Some sectors, however, appeared to be immune from layoffs, with many markets actually benefiting from increased spending on counter-terrorism. These areas will be described.

Security Checks—In the wake of September 11th an increasing number of companies are fingerprinting job applicants and checking with the Immigration and Naturalization Service to check on legal status. "This is probably the most security conscious we have been in the last 60 years," said Phil Anderson of the Center for Strategic and International Studies in Washington.

Everyone from temporary employees to food service workers is undergoing background checks. However, civil liberty groups are keeping a close watch on the increased security measures to ensure that workers' privacy rights are not violated and that illegal searches are not conducted. Doing criminal checks on every applicant also puts a strain on industries' financial resources. More on background checks in Chapter 7.

Where the Jobs Are

Government still offers multiple job opportunities, especially now that a lot of Baby Boomers are retiring. There are currently shortages of engineers, scientists, attorneys, and professional managers. Additionally, the government is expected to hire 16,000 information technology (IT) workers over the next few years. Check out the government's official Web site: www.usajobs.opm.gov, (the federal government's human resources agency) for information. The government Web site www.governmentguide.com, provides access to information about all types of government services throughout the country. At the site's Home Page just type in the desired zip code for local-specific information. This site also has a job center link.

The Federal Bureau of Investigation (FBI) plans to hire 900 Special Agents to handle the demands of fighting terrorism. To apply for an FBI job go to www.fbi.gov and select "Employment" or visit www.fbijobs.com to apply for a Special Agent position. To qualify you must be a U.S. citizen, at least 23 years old (and not older than 37), and in good physical condition. Special Agents earn $44,000 during training and up to $58,335 upon graduation from the academy.

Defense contractors are expected to earn hundreds of billions of dollars as the nation's wartime economy expands. Companies like Northrop Grumman have hundreds of positions open, and are expected to hire an additional 2,000 when suitable candidates can be found.

Security Jobs Are Hiring Now!

Security is a growing field with new job opportunities in private, government, and corporate settings. Directors of Security, who earned $90,000 before September 11th, are now making up to $400,000. Thousands of jobs are being created to bolster "homeland security." One agency that is receiving increased funding is the Immigration and Naturalization Service, currently hiring Border Patrol Agents, Immigration Inspectors, and District Adjudications Officers. To get more information about these positions go to their Web site: www.ins.usdoj.gov, or call the Job Information Line at (800) 238-1945 or (877) 375-3166. You may also apply by telephone at (888) 300-5500 (for border patrol jobs) or (877) 875-4879 (for immigration inspector jobs).

Following September 11th the federal government created a new agency, the Transportation Security Administration, to hire thousands of new professional airport transportation security screeners at 415 of the nation's commercial airports. These new hires are to be better trained and compensated than those in the past to ensure that security lapses in airports will be resolved.

The government is currently hiring over 60,000 persons for these positions:

- Supervisory Transportation Security Screeners—manage, train and supervise personnel that provide frontline security and protection of air travelers and airports. The salary range is from $36,400 to $56,400 depending on qualifications and experience.
- Transportation Security Screeners—provide frontline security and protection of air travelers, airports and airplanes; identify dangerous or deadly objects in baggage, cargo and on passengers. The salary range is from $23,600 to $35,400 depending on qualifications and experience.

To be considered for these airport security jobs you must be a U.S. citizen, have a high school education and undergo a variety of tests. You must be proficient in English, pass a background check, and undergo medical and physical examinations and a pre-employment drug test. Generous benefits such as health insurance, retirement, and paid leave are available with these positions.

For these and other transportation security jobs see: www.tsa.dot.gov/employment_opps/securityscreeners_index.shtm or for further assistance contact The Transportation Security Administration directly at www.tsa.gov/contacts/contact_us.shtm.

The **Central Intelligence Agency (CIA)** has been flooded with over 100,000 applications since 9/11, but few of the candidates have been sufficiently qualified. Although diversity has never been the CIA's strongest suit, Congress finally pushed for its reform and the agency has since actively recruited African Americans and other minorities. Even with this, however, minorities still only account for one of four CIA employees.

Clandestine operators are highly needed who, under the Directorate of Operations, would work to collect intelligence. Operator applicants fluent in foreign languages (especially Arabic and Farsi) are likely to receive special consideration.

At the CIA's official Web site, www.cia.gov/index.html access the following employment sectors: clandestine service (operations officers), scientists, engineers and technologists (satellite reconnaissance, IT managers, systems engineers, etc.), analytical positions (economist, counterterrorism and military analyst), language positions (Middle Eastern language specialist and foreign language instructor), and professional positions (the largest sector with openings for architects, facilities maintenance personnel, security officers, and physician's assistants).

To apply for a position with the CIA you must be a citizen of the United States and at least 18 years old. A college degree (especially an advanced one) will put you at the head of the line. There are two ways to apply for a job at the CIA. The preferred method is the online résumé submission   found   at   the   bottom   of   each   position   at www.cia.gov/cia/employment/ciaindex.htm.

For Clandestine Service Positions you may also mail your application to:

CST Division

P.O. Box 4605, Dept: Internet

Reston, VA 20195

For other CIA positions mail your résumé and cover letter to:

Recruitment Center

Attn: (fill in position applying for)

PO Box 4090, Dept: Internet

Reston, VA 20195

Current job benefits offered to CIA employees are paid time off, health and life insurance, retirement, education and training, health services, child care, and membership in a credit union. Drug abuse is one of the common reasons applicants are denied a security clearance, something you must get before an offer of employment will ever be extended.

Diversity and the CIA
"Our country is home to gifted people of virtually every national origin, creed, and culture. In our diversity there is tremendous strength. We must learn to recognize this diversity as the valuable asset that it is. If we fail to do so, we will waste an enormous amount of talent and resources. That is a waste which our country cannot afford and which I will not tolerate. I regard our diversity as a powerful tool that can help us meet the intelligence challenges of the coming century." George Tenet, Director of Central Intelligence, 1999 Statement on Diversity.

Other Promising Fields

Finance is faring well, particularly since interest rates are at their lowest in decades. Home refinancing has become increasingly popular with homeowners who want to cut their monthly payments. This has created jobs in the mortgage banking business.

Health Care is poised to be one of the hottest areas in the 21st century. There is a severe nursing shortage, and anyone skilled in nursing can pretty much write his or her own ticket anywhere in the country. Also in demand are pharmacists (especially for hospitals) and radiology technicians. (See Other Cool Hot Careers for more on a career in pharmacy). As the population ages, biotech and medical equipment manufacturers will expand their workforces. In the fall of 2002 Monster.com (www.monster.com) had over 5,000 jobs listed in the health care field.

Education offers multiple opportunities for teachers in every area of the country. Consider getting a teacher's certificate if you love growing young minds. The U.S. suffers a chronic shortage of hundreds of thousands of qualified teachers. A teachers' Web site containing a job bank and professional resources is www.teachersplanet.com. For teachers with special certifications (like special education or bilingual skills), there are more jobs than qualified applicants. Bilingual jobs can be found at www.bilingual-jobs.com, a site that prides itself on being "the premier diversity job destination for bilingual professionals."

Matchmaking

Before you decide which of the many jobs now in demand are right for you, you'll want to do more research. Figuring out what matters to you most will help you make the right choice. Although this has been covered before, your evaluation should include asking what kind of people you would like to serve, what kind of people you want to work with, and how the job requirements suit your interests and skills.

The U.S. Department of Commerce provides forecasts for selected manufacturing and service industries. Employment trends, sales, tax receipts, and ancillary activities generated by manufacturers are evaluated to make forecasts. For information about public and privately held companies, try Dun and Bradstreet and Standard and Poor's and Moody's directories. These publications are in your public library.

Other industry information resources include newspapers, online news, magazines like Business Week and Forbes, and trade magazines like Publishers Weekly. Check out www.Brint.com, a Website especially for researching companies.

Got Skills?

Twenty-first-century jobs in fields like high-speed communications, technology, and bioengineering require specially trained persons. There are many ways to get training that will help you open doors to these breakthrough fields. If you are currently employed, try to get your employer to provide training. Community colleges and job training centers often work with large corporations by offering various training programs to ensure companies have a trained workforce. To get a list of accredited trade and technical schools write the National Assn. of Trade and Technical Schools, 2521 Wisconsin Ave., NW, Washington, DC 20009, (202) 333-1021.

According to the U.S. Department of Labor, employers are looking for people with these types of skills:

- Problem-solving
- Human relations
- Teaching-training
- Money management
- Foreign language skills
- Vocational-Technical
- Computer programming
- Science and math
- Information management
- Business management

The Source's Apprentice

Because of increasing difficulty in finding skilled workers, the apprenticeship, an old-fashioned way of recruiting workers, is making a comeback. An apprenticeship is a working relationship between an employer and employee during which the employee learns a trade. Popular in the old days, this training method faded as people migrated to offices. An apprenticeship is one career route you might consider if you like working with your hands or doing what is known as "blue collar" work. But don't be misled by the term…many of these jobs pay very well.

Apprenticeships include on-the-job training and any other required instruction. The apprentice usually works under the supervision of a journey-worker, and the term can last one to six years.

Famous Apprentices
John Deere, of farm equipment fame, started out as a blacksmith's apprentice and later (in 1837) invented a revolutionary self-scouring steel plough that opened up the prairies to development. This invention led to the creation of a highly successful company. Another man whose apprenticeship helped launch a lucrative patent was Elias Howe, Jr., who invented the modern sewing machine (1846). Isaac Singer (the other sewing machine inventor) actually borrowed Howe's design to make the machine suitable for home use.

The U.S. Department of Labor issues certificates of completion upon completing a registered apprentice program. There are currently over 830 registered occupations like these:
- Electrician
- Carpenter
- Plumber
- Sheet metal worker
- Machinist
- Roofer
- Firefighter
- Bricklayer
- Cook/Chef
- Correction officer
- Automobile mechanic
- Welder
- Cement Mason
- Toolmaker

To apply for an apprenticeship write your local job service office (listed in the state government section of the telephone directory under Employment Service), join a union, or write:

The Bureau of Apprenticeship and Training
Employment and Training Administration
U. S. Department of Labor
200 Constitution Ave. NW
Washington, D. C. 20210

This bureau also has many regional offices in large cities where you can register in person.

Other Cool Hot Careers

Chef—Americans love to eat. TV cooking shows are extremely popular and there are a lot of Emeril-wannabes out there. If you love to cook, consider a career as a professional chef. The United States

Personal Chef Association at www.uspca.com can help you get the necessary training to become a personal chef. A more gossip-focused site that tracks celebrity chefs is www.greatchefs.com. There is a Job Finders bank at www.starchefs.com that also offers recipes and information about star chefs around the world.

Court Reporter—As long as there are courts there will be a need for transcripts of the proceedings. Court reporters earn a median salary of around $54,000 per year. Contact your local community college to enroll in classes or get information about jobs in your area. Or write the National Court Reporters Association, 8224 Old Courthouse Road, Vienna, VA 22181-3808, or call (703) 556-6272. Their Web site at www.verbatimreporters.com has information about distance learning and online test-taking for certifications.

Network Administrator—There is a big demand for network administrators. To learn more about this highly-paid profession, write the Institute for Certification of Computer Professionals, 2200 East Devon Avenue, Suite 268, Des Plaines, IL 60018 or visit Certification Magazine at www.certmag.com.

Paramedic—As cities grow, they must constantly improve their emergency response systems, and thus the demand for qualified emergency medical technician increases. This occupation is, however, not for the faint of heart. Talk to people in the field to get the inside scoop on what an EMT career is really like. Write the National Association of Emergency Medical Technicians, 102, West Leake Street, Clinton, MS 39056, (601) 924-7744 for information, or visit paramedic Chad Moser's site www.angelfire.com/ok/marvin1226 where real-life paramedics discuss their jobs without editorializing.

Personal Trainer—If you workout at a gym, you have probably noticed personal trainers assisting clients and hyperactive aerobics instructors leading a group in a sweat-drenched workout. Given that millions of Americans are trying to lose weight and get in shape, the field of fitness has many opportunities. Check out www.aerobics.com to get information on how to become a certified fitness trainer. In some of the larger cities personal trainers earn as much as $100.00 per hour.

Pharmacist—Pharmacists dispense drugs prescribed by physicians and provide information to patients about medications and their use. They must understand the composition and clinical effects of drugs. Most pharmacists work in a retail drug store, a hospital or clinic. Others specialize in drug therapies to treat cancer or mental illness and must ensure that harmful drug interactions do not occur. Prospective pharmacists should have scientific aptitude, good communication skills, and a desire to help others. A state license is required to practice. As the population ages, this field is expected to grow through 2010. Median annual earnings of pharmacists in 2000 were $70,950, although some earned as much as $89,000. For more information about a career in pharmacy, visit www.medoptions.com ("a healthcare personnel sourcing service") or contact the American Association of Colleges of Pharmacy, 1426 Prince St., Alexandria, VA 22314 (www.aacp.org) and the National Association of Boards of Pharmacy, 700 Busse Highway, Park Ridge, IL 60068 (www.nabp.net).

Webmaster—As the Internet continues to add thousands of new Web sites every month, there is a burgeoning demand for professional designers and maintainers of these sites. For more information and help on building an outstanding professional Web site, visit www.sitepoint.com.

E-training

E-training is an exciting new learning method using the Internet. E-training, also called distance learning and Web-based training, has grown beyond self-improvement tutorials like how to bake cakes and conversational French to include advanced degrees and Web certifications. Many of these classes are free. Companies like PowerEd.com, an "edu-commerce company", create courses for online universities at Web sites like Barnes & Noble and career sites like Procter and Gamble.

Revolutionizing the way people learn, e-learning has many advantages. The training is self-paced, needs-based, focused on competencies, and can be tailored to your learning style. Considering all the information resources at your fingertips, it behooves you to continuously train to maintain a marketable edge. Just be sure to align your training choices with your career goals.

Here are some E-learning web sites. Many of these courses, however, are designed for employees of large organizations and the technical-certification ones are usually fee-based.

www.bn.com—Barnes & Noble's online university (business and education courses)

www.capella.edu—over 500 online courses

www.classesusa.com

www.click2learn.com

www.ecollege.com

www.encarta.msn.com/elearning

www.fathom.com

www.horizonlive.com

www.learnittoday.com—computer courses

www.learnkey.com

www.learn2.com

www.primelearning.com—tuition: $25-50 per course

www.smartforce.com/

www.trainingserver.com—(technical courses)

The Hidden Job Market

"Today's workers need to forget jobs completely and look instead for work that needs doing—and then set themselves up as the best way to get that work done."
—William Bridges, career consultant

In most areas of the country, only about ten percent of job openings are advertised in the classified section of the newspaper. For the remainder of job openings there is an enormous hidden market. Unpublished jobs are usually better than advertised ones because they are seldom entry-level.

A great way to find hidden jobs is through trade and professional organizations. If you've never joined one, this may be a good time to do so. Two good sources to find trade and professional organizations are the U.S. Department of Labor's Bureau of Labor Statistics, *Occupational Outlook Handbook* and the *Encyclopedia of Associations*.

It's All About Connections

Employers often prefer the hidden market over conventional methods because, aside from saving money in advertising and time spent on paperwork, a referral from a network contact is more credible. Being recommended by a friend is more likely to open a door, and applicants who have done their research and discovered hidden jobs on their own are respected by many employers.

Tip: Read the business section of newspapers (like The Wall Street Journal) to find announcements of new business openings or companies expanding in new locations. A blurb in the paper about someone's promotion also means there's an opening (their old job). Companies that are awarded big contracts also need workers for the new projects.

We'll explore careers in the hospitality and travel industry in another chapter.

Don't Forget to Look Here

Other places to find hidden jobs are in trade journals, newsletters, bulletin boards, job hotlines, store windows, radio, TV, technical schools, and community colleges. Look at the Web sites of alumni organizations and professional associations. For example, local chapters of the American Society for Training and Development (ASTD) often have job postings at their Web sites.

CHAPTER 5

Put It in Writing

"Everyone is necessarily the hero of his own life story."
—John Barth, novelist

This chapter will show you the best ways to compose a professional employment résumé and cover letter that highlight your skills and accomplishments and stimulate interest in you. You will also create an electronic résumé, imperative in today's job market, and learn how to post it on the Internet.

A Powerful Marketing Tool

Your résumé, essentially a door opener, is a summary of professionally relevant information concerning yourself, and must sufficiently sell your qualifications to warrant an interview. Without an interview you can't get a job.

"Your résumé is only a snapshot that should support your career goals."
—Ron Tepper, résumé expert

A résumé should act as a reference guide for the interviewer. If important information is absent from your résumé, the interviewer won't be able to discern your key qualifications and accomplishments.

A well-written résumé acts as a road map, guiding the interviewer through your background with clearly marked signs that highlight your skills and expertise.

The Four Questions

Employers ask four basic questions when reviewing your résumé:

1. What do you want? (The Objective)
2. Why are you qualified to do it? (The Summary)
3. Where have you done it? (Experience section)
4. How well was it done? (Achievements)

There is no universal résumé format. However, the following guidelines may be helpful in writing your own résumé. It is always best to have a specific job in mind when creating your résumé. Read job descriptions, highlight the requirements, skills and qualifications, and try to reflect these areas in your résumé.

Résumés usually fall into one of these categories:

- administration
- education
- finance
- health
- human resources
- management
- marketing/promotions
- office support
- sales
- social work
- technical/computers
- miscellaneous/other/student

Should I Reveal I'm African-American?

The answer to this question is: It depends. Human resource managers say it's best to exclude personal information like racial or ethnic background. Also, a once popular practice of including photos with applications faded following passage of civil rights legislation in 1964, **making it illegal for employers to discriminate against an individual on the basis of race, color, religion, or national origin.** Many companies will not even consider interviewing anyone (especially a minority) who submits a personal photograph, because if your application is rejected they could be charged with racial discrimination. In our litigious-happy society, corporations fearful of getting sued are always trying to cover their backsides. (See the section "Post it on the Web" for the latest government rulings regarding applicants who post résumés on the Internet).

But What if the Employer is Black?

> *"No matter where you is or what you is, be what you is,*
> *'cause if you is what you ain't, you isn't."*
> —Bre'r Rabbit

With black-friendly or black-owned companies, however, it's a different story. If you are applying to a minority-owned company, you could mention your membership in black associations, black fraternities/sororities, and volunteer work at your black church. Let them figure it out. Companies are looking for workers who can easily fit into the corporate culture, and being black and applying to a black-owned company definitely gives you an advantage.

The First Go Round

You probably have a lot of questions about résumé preparation and format. For example, how many pages should it be? Should it contain personal data like height? Should it include salary history? The answers in a moment, but for now, know there are a right way and a wrong way to prepare a résumé.

From the Employer's Perspective

In a major corporation the average human resources manager or person responsible for hiring reads an estimated 20,000 résumés every year! This comes to about 75 résumés per day. Let's say Tanya, a personnel manager, is trying to fill a key position in her company and has begun accepting résumés. Not surprisingly, they arrive by the barrel and she has her hands full skimming them to select possible candidates for next week's interviews. At night she's pretty fatigued but must go through a whole new stack of fresh résumés. How does she get through this onslaught? Naturally, the first résumés she discards are those that are sloppy or difficult to read. Résumés reflect the personal style of the writer and a sloppy résumé is indicative of a sloppy person.

Tanya then checks to see if the requirements of the opening match the applicant's credentials. If not, the résumé is marked "no interest" and perhaps a "no thank you" letter is sent. Employers also try to disqualify applicants who may not be a good "fit" with their company. Texas Instruments uses something called a "fit checker" on its Web site to help job hunters decide whether to go ahead and submit a résumé.

Filters for Screening Résumés

As your résumé is reviewed it will be screened for:
- Sloppiness
- Illegibility
- Incompleteness
- Incompatibility with current openings, and
- Inadequate qualifications

While *scanning* (not reading) your résumé the typical manager asks, "Does this person have all the necessary qualifications?" The manager also reviews years of experience, your accomplishments, and how you compare with other candidates.

Résumé Formats

Most experts agree the perfect résumé has:

- strong content
- one page
- a professional layout
- an easy to read format
- quantifiable skills and actions

Chronological, Linear, or Functional?

Chronological—This résumé style, the traditional format, lists jobs in reverse chronological order. It shows how you've moved up the ladder and progressed in your field. This is probably the most popular format.

Linear—A variation of the chronological format, the linear style is relatively new. The difference between this and the chronological one is the Experience section is written on a line-by-line (hence linear) basis and in a narrative style. This highlights job responsibilities and accomplishments for easier reading.

Functional—The functional résumé places accomplishments and skills into groups to sell highlighted aptitudes. To get someone's attention you must accentuate your major achievements at the beginning of the résumé. Of all the types and above all, this résumé stresses *what* you do. A warning: employers sometimes scrutinize functional résumés more carefully since people use them to camouflage flaws or hide big gaps in employment. This type of résumé is also called analytical, skill-oriented, or creative.

Chronological

This résumé is divided into:

a) Heading—generally centered on the page, it should have your full name in all caps, complete address, home telephone number, and if you have them, e-mail address, cell phone and fax numbers.

b) Objective—This states what type of work you desire. Don't be vague or the employer will think you haven't given much thought to what you want to do.

c) Education—This should include schools attended, year graduated, degree(s) awarded, major and honors.

d) Experience—The experience part of your résumé is important because it must convince prospective employers that you are worthy of an interview. Experience should include the name of former employers, dates you worked, location, and type of company, etc. It should also contain your job title, what your responsibilities were, and any special accomplishments. (Hopefully, you compiled this information already). Take care with this section as it will act as a kind of background rehearsal for your interview.

Linear

This résumé has these key components:

a) Heading

b) Summary (of Qualifications)—spotlights enough of your credentials to whet the reader's appetite for more. It should be concise and relevant to the position. The purpose of the Summary section is to sell your strengths and convey the scope of your professional experience.

c) Experience

d) Education

e) Other (professional associations, publications, leadership roles, etc.)

Tip: Be sure the body of your résumé backs up all the statements in your summary.

Functional

The functional résumé attempts to catch the reader's eye from the beginning by stating major accomplishments and most relevant professional experience. This style is good if you're making a career change or trying to conceal job-hopping.

Functional résumés include:

a) Heading
b) Qualification Summary
c) Major accomplishments—this section highlights achievements in areas such as marketing or human resources. Use quantitative descriptions like: "Increased sales by 50% from $100,000 to $150,000 in the first year."
d) Work history—This section should be organized in reverse chronological order. It is not necessary to go back too many years, as employers are more interested in what you've done in the past five to seven years.
e) Education

The order can vary, but Education usually follows Work History unless it makes you more marketable to reverse the order.

Example of a Summary of Qualifications
• Highly motivated sales person breaking all previous company records for sales volume and client development. Demonstrated leader who constantly achieved objectives. Proven ability to effectively analyze markets, target areas of highest return, and develop strategies to attain sales goals.

Write It!

It's time to put all of this information to use and write your résumé.

Since a résumé is only a brief summary of your professional background, it needs to show your skills and work history in a clear, concise format that is attractive and easy to read.

Following are some tips for composing your résumé. There will be some samples at the end of the chapter.

Length

A well-written résumé is brief. However, individuals with more than ten years' experience will find it difficult to squeeze their professional qualifications on one page. For most people, two pages are adequate.

Note: A Curriculum Vitae is a longer, more comprehensive summary of experience, accomplishments and published works and will not be covered in this volume.

Appearance is everything

The résumé's appearance is very important. Don't try to stand out by being cutesy or unorthodox. Do not put pictures of animals or religious symbols on your résumé.

Tall Tales

Be careful if you exaggerate accomplishments because the fibs *will* catch up with you. Many managers now use an interviewing technique called "patterning" to uncover inconsistencies that suggest exaggeration or dishonesty. This means asking related questions at different times during the interview to catch patterns that don't fit.

Hobbies and Extracurricular Activities

People put hobbies on a résumé to suggest a well-rounded person with interests outside of work. If this information does not help the employer better understand your abilities or directly relate to your qualifications for the position you seek, then leave it off. Do not list what magazines to which you subscribe. Avoid including any information that might somehow alienate you, such as announcing you are a vegetarian or religious freedom fighter.

Personal Data

Information that is not considered job-relevant should be omitted. As for putting marital status, if you're young, female and married, you risk employers wondering if you're going to start having children and be on maternity leave next year. It's none of their business.

Salary History

There are several good reasons why you shouldn't include salary history or requirements on your résumé. One, it is considered to be in poor taste and two, may give the impression that you are only interested in money. You don't want to draw attention to how much you *cost* but rather your *value*. Provide salary history only in a cover letter if asked to do so by the employer. Finally, disclosing your salary requirements, if higher than the employer wants to pay, might cause you to be screened out of a job you are really interested in. You can negotiate salary later.

Accentuate the Positive

Employers are looking for individuals who can add value to their organization. When writing your résumé, try to do so in a way that reveals how you solve problems, lead and motivate others, and are cost conscious on-the-job.

Writing Style

Avoid redundancy and never use the pronoun "I." Use quantitative descriptions (e.g. developed strategies that led to a 60% increase in sales) and brief phrases rather than complete sentences. Begin with an action verb (e.g. supervised staff of five).

Paper

Stick to white or ivory-colored high-quality paper. If your paper is cheap or flimsy, the employer might get the wrong impression of you.

References

Employment consultants suggest not providing references, because if they're checked and negative information is disclosed, it may disqualify you for an interview and you won't have a chance to correct any bad impressions. Most employers wait to check references after an offer of employment is imminent. Remember to get permission from and alert your references if they may be called upon. With their permission, you may coach references about what you would like them to say about you should they be asked to do so. If you think a reference might say anything negative, no matter how seemingly insignificant, consider removing that name from your reference list.

Hint: It is not necessary to use the phrase "references upon request." Employers know references will be provided if requested.

More Tips

Managers are busy and don't have time to waste. Employment experts claim that 95% of all interviews are granted only after the company has received and read the candidate's résumé. This is considered to be a "negative" screen process. If you have a poorly prepared résumé, you will be screened out before you even get a foot in the door. Your résumé is a permanent record of your work history and strengths, and so prepare it with that in mind.

Keep it Clean

Proofread copies of your résumé carefully for clarity, typos, and misspelled words. Ask a friend to do the same. Good grammar and spelling are essential.

So, how will you know if your résumé is working? If it gets you an interview. You have about 15 seconds to sell yourself to the reader.

Action Words

Each description of your job task should begin with an action verb that says what you did. Here is a partial list to help you get started.

accelerated	evaluated	mastered	provided	simplified
accomplished	expanded	motivated	proficient in	set up
achieved	expedited	operated	purchased	solved
adapted	facilitated	ordered	recommended	structured

administered	found	originated	reduced	streamlined
analyzed	generated	organized	reinforced	supervised
approved	increased	participated	reorganized	supported
conceived	influenced	performed	revamped	surpassed
conducted	implemented	planned	revised	taught
completed	initiated	pinpointed	reviewed	trained
controlled	instructed	prepared	scheduled	translated
coordinated	interpreted	produced	used	created
improved	programmed	utilized	delegated	inspected
proposed	demonstrated	launched	proved	won
wrote	designed	led	developed	directed
maintained	earned	managed	effected	established
motivated	negotiated	upgraded		

Nouns and Modifiers: ability, competent, effectiveness, qualified, technical, actively, competence, pertinent, resourceful, versatile, capacity, consistent, proficient, substantially, vigorous.

A Résumé Template

Start gathering information you want to put in your résumé. To do this look at the following topics: work experience, educational background, special skills, volunteer experience, military duty, and interests. You might want to record these on different sheets of paper for each position. It might look something like this:

WORK EXPERIENCE

Name of Employer: _____

Starting date: _____

Salary: _____

Termination date: _____

Type of company: _____

Job title: _____

Supervisor's name: _____

Duties you performed: _____

Skills you used: _____

Greatest accomplishments: _____

What you liked most: _____

What you liked least: _____

Reason for leaving: _____

EDUCATIONAL BACKGROUND

Name of school or training program: _____

City and State: _____

Dates attended: _____

Certificate or diploma received: _____

Major (and/or minor): _____

Grade point average: _____

Awards or scholarships: _____

SPECIAL SKILLS

Computer skills: _____

Office skills: _____

Technical skills: _____

Foreign languages: _____

VOLUNTEER EXPERIENCE

Name of organization: _____

Your title or role: _____

Dates: _____

Type of organization: _____

Work performed (skills used): _____

What you learned from the experience: _____

MILITARY EXPERIENCE

Branch of service: _____

Rank: _____

Dates: _____

Special skills or training: _____

INTERESTS

List interests and hobbies that would be a good match for the particular job you are seeking.

Sample Résumé

This sample résumé is for someone without a lot of experience trying to enter a new field.

JERMAINE HAWKINS
1234 Grand Ave.
Dallas, TX 75201
(214) 555-6789

OBJECTIVE:	An entry level X-ray technologist position in a health care facility where I can utilize my training and education
EDUCATION:	El Centro Community College, Dallas, TX
2000-2001	A.A.S. X-ray Technologist Program, 2001
1999	Southland Training Institute, Dallas, TX
	Certificate in MS Office (Excel, Word, Access)

VOLUNTEER EXPERIENCE: Routh Street Clinic, Dallas, TX, 1999-2002—Intern
- Assisted staff in the X-ray department in preparing and processing patient X-rays
- Input patient data into computer system
- Interacted with patients in a courteous, helpful manner
- Interviewed patients regarding their personal and medical history

EXPERIENCE: Tasty Steak House, Fort Worth, TX 1995-1999—Busboy
- Maintained the cleanliness of all tables and linens
- Set tables with clean linen and silverware
- Assisted with washing and disinfecting dishes and glassware
- Provided general cleanup of restaurant after hours

COMMUNITY INVOLVEMENT: Goodwill Baptist Church, Arlington, TX 1999-2002
- Assisted youth group during recreational outings

SKILLS: Conversational Spanish

Note: Education was put first to highlight recent certification in the line of work sought by job hunter. Also, volunteer experience precedes work history because of its relevance to the objective.

E-Résumés

With the rise of digital technology, employers have embraced electronic résumés as the résumé standard. This is partly due to the surging popularity of e-mail as a business communication tool. An electronic résumé, also known as an e-résumé, is a document that can be transmitted electronically through the Internet to an employment database, an employer's Web site, or to an individual's e-mail address. There are three types of electronic résumés: ones that can be e-mailed, attached as an ASCII file, or scanned. ASCII résumés (see below) are popular because they're universally readable. According to employers, e-mailed plain-text résumés are the preferred format, followed by scannable résumés printed on white paper and mailed. Keep in mind that faxed résumés do not always scan well.

Scannability

Today, because of the sheer volume of résumés received, companies scan résumés with computer programs. Unless intentionally pulled out of the database, a human rarely reads the résumé. Résumés are scanned for key words that indicate skills, education, and knowledge that the employer seeks. Be sure and include scannable key words that are part of the actual job description. Typical key words people use to have their résumé selected are managed, supervised, directed, and created, etc. Do not send your résumé as an e-mail attachment unless the format you're using (e.g. Microsoft Word) is specifically requested. Use a scannable résumé when you send a paper résumé to an employer or when an employer asks you to fax a résumé.

ASCII Résumés

A complex network like the Internet with millions of people and thousands of companies exchanging information calls for a standard, common text language that allows different word processing applications to communicate. This common text language is known as ASCII (pronounced "askee") text. There is no formatting in ASCII documents, thus allowing you to create an online résumé all employers can view no matter what computer software they are using. A detailed explanation of how ASCII works is beyond the scope of this book, but it is basically a code that assigns numeric values to letters, numbers, and other characters.

How to Create an ASCII Résumé

Choose an ASCII or plain-text résumé
- when you e-mail a résumé to an employer
- when you post online at employment sites
- when someone asks you to e-mail a résumé
- when a job advertisement lists an e-mail address

Here are the steps for creating a basic electronic résumé (plain-text or ASCII résumé).

- Open a word processing document; make sure margins are set at 0 and 65 (many computer monitors only display 60 to 65 characters)
- Name and save the document
- Select a font like Times New Roman or Courier of at least 12-point type size
- Type in your résumé, everything flush left, using all caps to highlight your name and major headings. Don't indent or use tabs (they'll be lost when converted to ASCII)
- Spell-check your résumé and have someone else proofread
- Save your résumé as a Rich Text Format (RTF) document which should be a "Save" or "Save As" option

Do not use special characters or mathematical symbols. ASCII résumés have no formatting, special characters, tabs, underlining, bolding, or special fonts.

Web Résumé

A web résumé is a résumé you can place on the Internet. It looks like a paper résumé but often contains graphics. If samples of your work are attached to the résumé it is called a Web portfolio. You don't normally send a Web résumé to an employer but rather list your Web address on the e-résumé or paper résumé you send. Choose a Web résumé/portfolio if you work in a creative field like music and you want to include sound clips from recent performances, or you want to signify that you are computer literate and on the cutting edge.

Sample Electronic Résumé

YOUR NAME
ADDRESS
CITY, STATE ZIP CODE
Telephone: (123) 555-9999
Fax: (123) 555-7890
E-mail: Yourname@email.com
www.yourURL.com
Objective: State what you want to do or what you are qualified to do.
Summary of Qualifications: This is a keyword summary listing nouns that describe your skills.
PROFESSIONAL EXPERIENCE:
2000—Present—Employer, location, job title
List accomplishments and skills, noting your actions and the results of your actions. Use nouns and noun phrases to describe tasks, special projects, etc.
1998—2000—Employer, location, job title
List accomplishments as above.

1996—1998—Employer, location, job title and so on
EDUCATION
List your educational achievements and include professional certifi-
cations and training.

Post It on the Web

To find Web sites where you can post your résumé refer to the sites
listed in Chapter 3 or use one of the search engines to find your own
sites. Once you have found a good Web site, read the instructions for
how to post a résumé. Normally, you type your name, address, phone
and E-mail address, and then paste a copy of your résumé to the desig-
nated space. To copy and paste your résumé

-   Open your plain-text or ASCII résumé and highlight the entire
    résumé
-   Go to Edit menu and choose copy (or right-click mouse and
    choose copy)
-   Switch to your e-mail program
-   Create a new e-mail message
-   Place your cursor inside the e-mail message area
-   Right-click and choose Paste or choose Paste from Edit menu
-   Send it

For more information on writing and posting e-résumés, read
Internet Résumés, by Peter D. Weddle.

Racial Profiling of Online Résumés

When Lockheed Martin Aeronautics Company won a contract to
build the next generation of stealth aircraft, it received more than
100,000 résumés over the Internet within a week. Every day, tens of millions of résumés are transmitted electronically. This technology has
obvious merits but poses problems for employers trying to comply with
federal anti-discrimination rules.

Companies with more than 100 employees are required by the government to collect demographic data (like race, gender, and ethnicity) from applicants to ensure that new hires yield a diverse work force. Applications received by companies must be retained for two years. Although companies often ask demographic-based questions, responding to them is always voluntary, thus making it difficult, if not impossible, to produce accurate diversity numbers.

This information-gathering challenge worsened in the mid-1990s with the rise of the Internet and after the U.S. Department of Labor determined that an applicant is anyone who submits a résumé online. Given the enormous volume of résumés exchanged today, it is almost impossible to comply with the Labor Department's ruling. The dispute is now about what constitutes an application. Stakeholders in this argument are asking two primary questions:

- Should all electronically-submitted résumés be considered true applicants (even with new software that allows job seekers to flood the market with résumés)?
- If demographic information is not voluntarily disclosed, should the company try to guess an applicant's race based on name, address, or some other profile indicator?

"The whole thing is a joke," said Jeffrey Norris of the Equal Employment Advisory Council, a Washington trade group of 350 major U.S. corporations that believes job applicants should be those who qualify and have actually been considered for a job. Other employers affected by this rule claim they cannot possibly gather information on hundred of thousands of applicants, arguing that applicants are not so until actually interviewed for a position.

At the end of 2000, the U.S. Office of Management and Budget ordered the Equal Employment Opportunity Commission, along with other federal agencies, to update the definition of job applicant. "It's just not practical to have to count every single person who sends in a résumé over the Internet," Norris said. (Source: New York Times, 09/22/02).

Cover Letters

To avoid having to modify your résumé for every potential job, you need a good cover letter that customizes your connection to the specific job requirements. A cover letter is your opportunity to sell yourself to the employer. Use it to introduce yourself, expand upon your résumé, and highlight your skills and accomplishments. The cover letter also serves to demonstrate your knowledge of the industry and how your experience relates to the position. You should *always* attach a cover letter to every résumé you send out—no exceptions.

Note: Not all experts agree cover letters are important. Some argue that managers pay little attention to cover letters because of all the résumés they must read, and cover letters add little meaningful information. And since many are "broadcast" letters, i.e. used by the applicant to mass mail his or her résumé to a lot of prospective employers, the letter loses a personal touch. I believe, however, that cover letters are important and urge you to use them.

Types of Letters

Cover letters, like résumés, should be clear and concise. Their purpose is to make the hiring authority more receptive to talking with you. Don't forget to proofread your cover letters for errors. A poorly written cover letter can ruin your chances for employment.

There are four types of cover letters:

1. **Broadcast** (unsolicited) letter to employers—sent as part of a mass mailing; not particularly effective with maybe a 2 to 5% response.
2. **Broadcast letter to search firms**—sent also to employment agencies; is more detailed and often includes salary requirements.

3. **Response to advertisements**—this is a letter of application and always refers to the position and publication where the ad appeared.
4. **Personal referral (networking) letter**—don't forget to mention the referring person and your relationship; make this letter friendlier and more personal.

Letter Format
- Paragraph one states what job you're applying for
- Paragraph two should match your skills and experience with those required for the job
- Paragraph three closes the letter with a thank you and promise to follow up with a phone call.

Letter Guidelines
- always address the letter to the person authorized to hire
- know something about the company you're contacting
- be warm, friendly and enthusiastic
- identify one thing about yourself that's unique and relevant to the job
- be specific about what position you're applying for
- be brief

Sample Response to an Ad

July 14, 2002
Mr. Joe Smith
Human Resources Manager
XYZ Company
Big Town, U.S.A. 12345
Dear Mr. Smith:

Your ad in the July 12th issue of the St. Louis Dispatch for a warehouse supervisor intrigues me because it sounds as though it were written for me.

As you can see from my enclosed résumé, I have the communication, problem solving, and other skills and experience that you are looking for. My five years of warehouse experience include supervising a forklift crew and handling all payroll functions. What my résumé cannot convey, of course, is my diligence and dedication to excellence.

I am confident that I can do the job and would like to meet with you to explore this matter further. I appreciate your consideration and will call next Friday to see if there is any additional information you would like to have.

Sincerely,

Clarence P. Job Hunter

What about Faxing My Résumé?

If you've been asked to fax your résumé be sure to send a hard copy by mail in case the print gets blurred during transmission. You want them to have a clean copy for their records.

Job Search / Résumé Log

A Job Search and Résumé Log help keep track of sent résumés and contacts.

Date Contacted/ Résumé Sent	Organization	Name/Title/ph#	Contact Source	Position Sought	Remarks/Notes
10/14/02	XYZ Company	Joe Smith, HR Manager (555) 123-4567	Mr. Smith's nephew Sam	Warehouse supervisor	Follow-up call 10/21/02

CHAPTER 6

Affirmative Action, Discrimination Laws, and Employment Agencies

"The most important thing is to be whatever you are without shame."
—Rod Steiger, actor

Affirmative action programs were originally created to open previously-closed doors to African-American workers. A brief history of this controversial subject will be covered in this chapter. You will learn where to find answers to questions about federal anti-discrimination laws. Is there a way you can benefit from affirmative action programs? Do any companies still openly use affirmative action? What is the difference, if any, between affirmative action and diversity?

Racism in Corporate America
Racism has been an intrinsic part of America's culture and heritage, and for a long time blacks were excluded from many employment, educational, and housing opportunities. Following the Civil War, during Reconstruction in the nineteenth century, blacks tried to find employment, but discriminatory job patterns prevailed and African Americans were relegated to low-skilled occupations. The rise of Jim Crow laws in

the late 19th century altogether institutionalized the segregation of blacks and whites in public accommodations like trains, locker rooms, drinking fountains, and workplaces. "Colored" water fountains and dressing rooms became the norm.

> *"We've seen America get comfortable with its prejudices."*
> —Nat Alston, Nat'l Assn. of African-Americans in Human Resources

Later, at the turn of the 20th century, black women found new professional opportunities as teachers. Black men continued to work in factories and in agricultural occupations. During World War II, new job opportunities opened for blacks only to evaporate at the war's end. When white soldiers returned to their old jobs, their previous seniority superseded black jobholders and the policy, "last hired, first fired," was common. Throughout the 1950s and 1960s, blacks even battled with organized labor over racist policies, and the NAACP worked hard to eliminate discrimination in labor unions.

Out of the Kitchen and Into the Streets

When Rosa Parks was arrested in December 1955 for refusing to give up her seat on the bus, the entire black population of Montgomery, Alabama started an unprecedented boycott of public transit that surprised the entire country. The transit boycott was eventually a success and out of it grew a new organization, the Southern Christian Leadership Conference (SCLC) and the eventual rise of Martin Luther King, Jr. The black protest movement finally began gathering some real momentum and would gain steam throughout the turbulent decade to follow. This battle clearly was not going to be won overnight.

What do we want? JOBS! When do we want them? NOW!

"Prejudice is a raft onto which the shipwrecked mind clambers and pad-
dles to safety."
—Ben Hecht, reporter and novelist

In the 1960s civil rights groups began demanding specific and quantifiable goals for achieving diversity in the workplace. During the 1960 presidential election, discussion of civil rights became a platform issue. Although Kennedy was actually a lukewarm supporter of civil rights, he finally saw the light after winning the election with the help of African-American voters, and eventually passed executive orders (rather than risking the wrath of a conservative Congress) to prohibit discrimination in federal employment. The long struggle for racial integration finally resulted in landmark legislation passed by President Johnson in 1964.

1964, a Watershed Year

"You do not take a person who, for years, has been hobbled by chains and
liberate him, bring him to the starting line of the race, and then say you
are free to compete with all the others, and still just believe that you have
been completely fair. We seek not just freedom, but opportunity."
—President Lyndon Johnson

Job discrimination was one of the central themes of the civil rights movement. Black civil rights groups, frustrated by white liberals' timid approach to passing legislation prohibiting discrimination, began demanding substantive action. Asking America to "close the springs of racial poison," President Johnson signed into law the Civil Rights Act of 1964 prohibiting discrimination against any individual "because of race, color, religion, sex, or national origin." With this new law on their side, civil rights activists began working with federal agencies to bring their workplaces into compliance. Thus began a slew of executive actions passed banning job discrimination. These new programs were called affirmative action.

Affirmative Action

Affirmative action has three primary objectives: 1) to overcome discrimination, 2) to increase workforce diversity, and 3) to reduce poverty among discrimination victims. (Source: Weiss, Robert, *We Want Jobs: A History of Affirmative Action*). By the end of President Nixon's term in office (1973), courts around the country mandated affirmative action programs. This did not, however, mean people automatically accepted affirmative action. By President Carter's term in office (1977) opposition to affirmative action began in earnest. Precipitating the rise of the new conservative movement, Reagan's administration in the 1980s was downright hostile to affirmative action. "Job quotas" became new targets of the right wing.

Preferential Racism?

> *"Prejudice is being down on something you're not up on."*
> —Anonymous

In recent years affirmative action's opponents have proclaimed the unfairness of such programs—that they are a "betrayal of U.S. individualism." Conservatives argue that affirmative action policies are racist because they categorize people by race or ethnicity. (Of course, they've probably never suffered discrimination or been denied a job because of their skin color). Supreme Court Justice Clarence Thomas, countering the black mainstream opinion, suggested that affirmative action demeans those it proposes to help, because they would never know if they got there on their own merits or because of "preferential treatment." It has been said that Justice Thomas himself has benefited from exactly the type of affirmative action policies he denigrates.

"Reverse Discrimination"

One famous reverse discrimination case involved Allan Bakke, a white man who applied for admission to a medical school in California but was rejected. Allegedly, Bakke's spot went to a less qualified minority candidate. Having higher test scores than some of the minority candidates who were in fact accepted, Bakke sued, claiming his constitutional rights were violated. The Supreme Court ruled that the quota system used by this medical school was discriminatory.

Efforts to roll back affirmative action continue by people who argue that "social engineering" and "big government" have no place solving these problems. President Clinton, upon taking office, held a pro-affirmative action position with a twist: "Mend it, but don't end it." Clinton listed four criteria for future affirmative action programs: 1) quotas would not be established, 2) no unqualified individuals would be hired, 3) there would be no reverse discrimination, and 4) programs would be terminated when they had achieved their goals.

So Who Benefited?

> *"We must learn to live together as brothers or perish together as fools."*
> —Martin Luther King, Jr.

For African-Americans, affirmative action had its biggest impact on blue-collar workers in the tobacco, steel, textile, construction industries, and for public employees like firefighters and police officers. The future of affirmative action is uncertain, and racial inequality in the workplace persists. Corporate leaders and managers must do everything in their power to change their cultures so that discrimination becomes obsolete. Some companies now even provide cultural sensitivity training to shatter racial stereotypes and demonstrate the power of inclusiveness. Smart companies know that diversity is good for business.

If Your Opportunities Aren't Exactly Equal

Title VII of the Civil Rights Act of 1964 forbids employers from discrimination against any person on the basis of sex, age, race, national origin or religion. The United States Equal Employment Opportunity Commission is the regulatory agency responsible for enforcing this federal law. Keep this law in mind during interviews, especially if the interviewer asks illegal questions about ethnicity and race. Sample illegal questions can be found in Chapter 8.

What should you do if you feel that you have been discriminated against? Any individual who believes that his or her employment rights have been violated may file a charge of discrimination with EEOC (see Web site below). If someone wishes to file a complaint without disclosing their identity, they may do so through another individual, organization or agency. A charge of discrimination may be filed by mail or in person at the nearest EEOC office or by calling the toll-free number below. The charge must be filed within 180 days of the alleged violation, but this can be extended to 300 days if the charge is covered by other state or local anti-discrimination laws.

> _"A man can't ride you unless your back is bent."_
> —Martin Luther King, Jr.

After a complaint has been filed with EEOC the employer is notified that a charge has been filed. There are several ways the charge can be handled to determine if a violation has occurred, all of which are described at the EEOC Web site. If discrimination has been found following a thorough investigation, remedies include back pay, promotion, reinstatement, hiring, other actions to make the individual "whole," payment of attorneys' fees, and other court costs.

To order publications about how these laws are enforced write, call, or fax:

U. S. Equal Employment Opportunity Commission
P.O. Box 12549

Cincinnati, OH 45212-0549
www.eeoc.gov
1-800-669-4000 or 1-800-669-3362
1-800-669-6820 (TTY)
1-513-489-8692 (fax)

Discrimination complaints may also be filed with the U.S. Department of Justice (Civil Rights Division)—www.usdoj.gov

The EEOC Web site has extensive information about discrimination laws and answers to almost every employment question imaginable.

For information about programs benefiting minority applicants read Willis L. Johnson's *Directory of Special Programs for Minority Group Members: Career Information Services, Employment Skills Banks, Financial Aid Sources*, 4th ed. Garrett Park Press, P.O. Box 190, Garrett Park, MD 20896.

Employment Agencies / Temping

Employment agencies are in business to match job hunters with prospective employers. Agencies solicit corporate clients to find job vacancies and then recruit prospective workers to fill open positions with client companies. Most of these agencies work on a commission basis, meaning they don't get paid until you accept the job and sign the dotted line. Since there are so many employment agencies, several specialize in particular fields like accounting, manual labor or technical. Before you register with an agency, talk to the placement manager to get a feel for how they operate. Understand the fee arrangements before you sign any contracts. Many positions are "applicant-paid fee" positions meaning you pay the commission if the agency secures you a job (commissions are usually based on a percentage of the annual salary and can be more than $3,000). Employment agencies spend a large part of their day "cold calling" companies to see if there are openings, or trying to sell the company on a particular applicant. If you have access to a telephone you can make these kinds of calls on your own. Unless you really don't know how to search the job market or don't have a lot of time, then use an employment agency only as a last resort. In another fee arrangement called "employer-paid fee," the employer pays the commission (or reimburses you), but you often have to stay in the job for a minimum of six months to one year.

Temping

While companies lay off employees (downsizing) to cut costs (and please their stockholders), they often turn right around and rehire as temporary workers the former employees that have been laid off. In this arrangement the company benefits financially by not having to pay benefits.

Temporary work used to be mostly low-paying, but today over one million temp jobs are available in all employment areas. Many job hunters like temping because they can get a feel for work environments and explore possible new job leads. Additionally, companies like using temps as a kind of audition before extending an offer. The benefits to temping are learning new skills (especially computer skills), getting a weekly paycheck, and networking. However, some temp jobs can be monotonous like filing, data entry or unloading boxes.

Open your Yellow Pages to "Employment-Contractors-Temporary Help" to find agencies that can help you get temporary assignments. Most of these staffing firms will also help you find permanent or temp-to-hire work. Some of the bigger temporary employment agencies are Manpower, Kelly, and Snelling. Many of these now permit you to apply online.

CHAPTER 7

Non-Corporate, Overseas and Government Jobs

In this chapter you will learn about opportunities to work outside the corporate world. There are scads of jobs with the federal government, abroad, on cruise ships, with not-for-profit organizations, as a volunteer and, for risk-takers, as an entrepreneur.

"America's technology has turned upon itself; its corporate form makes it the servant of profits, not the servant of human needs."
—Robin Morgan, author of Sisterhood is Powerful

Working for the Feds

The federal government is the nation's largest employer with over 3 million employees and is responsible for maintenance of highways, pollution control, air traffic, border security, disease control, and food safety. Some of the new security-related jobs were covered in an earlier chapter. African-Americans currently make up around 17% of the federal workforce, one-third of which are clerical jobs. However, according to the U.S. Labor Bureau, the *greatest opportunities for blacks in years ahead will be in computer and telecommunications with computer-related jobs expected to grow by 90%.* The government's challenge today is to retain workers by keeping salaries and benefits competitive with the private sector. Here are some benefits and drawbacks to working for the government.

Benefits

- Jobs are often state-of-the art projects like energy resource enhancement, crop development or cancer eradication.
- Most (85%) federal jobs are located outside Washington, D.C. so there are federal jobs all over the world.
- Rewards are generous with rapid promotion, advancement and other benefits like paid holidays
- Workforce diversity is higher in federal agencies than in the private sector
- You are often serving the greater good

Drawbacks

- Being a major government bureaucracy, things take longer to accomplish
- Salaries are sometimes lower than in the private sector
- Huge federal agencies have large hierarchies
- Imperfect work environments with old desks and chairs, poor ventilation, and shortage of equipment, especially up-to-date computers
- Poor job security; agencies face budget cuts
- Public disfavor; not everyone likes the government

How to Find Government Job Openings

These government publications describing current job openings are available by subscription and in libraries.

1. Federal Career Opportunities (FCO)
   P.O. Box 1059
   Vienna, VA 22183-1059
   (703) 281-0200

2. Federal Jobs Digest
   325 Pennsylvania Ave., SE
   Washington, DC 20003
   (800) 543-3000
   Note: Most federal agencies have their own job hotline numbers.

USAJOBS

To find and apply for federal jobs, the U.S. Office of Personnel Management has created USAJOBS (www.usajobs.opm.gov). USAJOBS provides worldwide job vacancies, employment information, job application forms, and online résumé posting. It is accessible 24/7 via computer or telephone. Another terrific Web site is www.fedworld.gov that "makes it easy to locate government information." You can find job openings and browse over 30 million government papers.

Touch Screen Computer Kiosk—Self-service information centers are located in federal buildings nationwide.

Automated Telephone System—An interactive voice response telephone system can be reached at (912) 757-3000 or TDD (912) 744-2299 and at 17 service centers throughout the country (listed in the Blue Pages).

You may apply for most jobs by sending a résumé or using the Optional Application for Federal Employment (OF-612—downloadable at Web site). If you don't use an OF-612 form, the following information must be included with your application:

- Job information—announcement number, title and grade
- Personal information—full name, address, day/evening phone numbers, social security number, country of citizenship, veterans' status
- Education—if some college but no degree, show credits earned
- Work Experience—job title, duties, accomplishment, employer's name and address, supervisor's name and phone number, starting/ending dates, salary, and whether your current supervisor may be contacted

- Other qualifications—job related training courses, special skills, licenses, honors, and awards, etc.

Background Checks

Some federal jobs require a security clearance involving a background investigation. Your personal habits will be scrutinized, drug tests conducted (see next section), and in some cases your neighbors and associates interviewed. Given heightened concerns over security following the 9/11 tragedy, many companies are beefing up employment screening practices. Investigators now routinely look at education records, arrest, court or criminal records, credit reports or bankruptcy filings, driving records and vehicle registrations, medical records and workers' compensation, military service records, property ownership, state licensing records, character references, and employment verification. Pre-employment screenings that cost $200 not long ago now cost roughly $50 because of improved technology.

Agency heads must be careful, however, when investigating minority candidates so as not to appear to be discriminatory. People of Middle Eastern descent have complained that they are suffering increased racial profiling since 9/11. Legal trouble is imminent if it appears people are singled out arbitrarily (by appearance) than for just cause. Additionally, an increasing number of companies are reluctant to answer detailed questions in a reference check about past employees due to the increased number of lawsuits from former employees. Now when queried, companies often provide only the dates of employment and positions held. For further information on federal protections for worker privacy rights look at the Fair Credit Reporting Act of 1971 (with multiple amendments in the late 1990s), the Privacy Act of 1974 and the Americans with Disabilities Act of 1990, among others. If you feel a background check was unfairly conducted, contact an employment attorney.

Drug Testing

Another possible condition for employment is pre-employment drug testing. This growing practice in businesses and schools has raised privacy issues. Those demanding less intrusive government consider drug testing a violation of the Fourth Amendment to the United States Constitution. Strict constitutionalists warn that the gradual erosion of civil liberties is akin to dropping a live frog into warm versus boiling water. In the latter, the frog is understandably alarmed enough to quickly hop out of the water...but in the former, is lulled into submission. You must decide for yourself if you will consent to invasions of privacy for whatever purpose.

The Fourth Amendment to the U. S. Constitution

"The right of the people to be secure in their persons, houses, papers, and effects, against unreasonable searches and seizures, shall not be violated, and no Warrants shall issue, but upon probable cause, supported by Oath or affirmation, and particularly describing the place to be searched, and the persons or things to be seized."

Why is pre-employment drug testing so important to business today? Because government studies reveal that 74% of all drug abusers are employed and that one out of six workers has a drug problem. On average these drug abusers are absent up to 16 times more often; are 1/3 less productive; cost an employer $7,000 to $10,000 per employee annually; and cost 300% more in medical costs.

Detection

According to CollegeGrad.com alcohol can be detected in the body for up to 24 hours whereas anabolic steroids and marijuana (THC) can be detected for up to 30 days. Most drug testing firms now use what is called a "Ten-Screen" test for cannabinoids (marijuana, hashish), cocaine, opiates (heroin, opium, codeine, morphine), amphetamines (speed), phencyclidine (PCP, angel dust), barbiturates, methaqualone (qualuudes), benzodiazepines (valium, xanax, halcyon, rohpynol, etc.), methadone, and propoxyphene (Darvon). There are newer tests for ethanol (alcohol), LSD, and other hallucinogens like psilocybin and MDMA, and inhalants (toluene, xylene, benzene). (Source: www.col-legegrad.com).

One of the leading drug testing companies, Psychomedics uses FDA-approved hair analysis to test for dozens of illicit substances. (www.pre-employmentdrugtests.com) If you do not use drugs but fail a drug screening anyway, tell the employer you do not use drugs and ask for a confirmation test. Some over-the-counter medications can cause false positive results including: Midol, Nuprin (ibuprofen), Sudafed, Vicks Nasal Spray, Neosynephrine, Ephedrine-based products (diet pills), and Vicks 44. If your request for a confirmation test is rejected because of the expense, offer to pay for the test. If the employer still balks at retesting, you may consult an attorney for legal counsel.

Jobs Abroad

Do you love to travel to exotic places? Have you ever considered living in a foreign country? It may sound glamorous, but not everyone is suited for overseas work. Leaving home for a job thousands of miles away in a foreign country can be traumatic. But for some, working abroad would be a dream fulfilled. There are hundreds of thousands of jobs in just about every country on the planet. First ask yourself if working abroad is aligned with your values and career goals. If you've determined that overseas work is right for you, the next step is to identify prospective employers that hire Americans for overseas positions. You can find these employers in the book *American Jobs Abroad* (see Recommended Reading), with company profiles and data about the countries in which they operate, the product/service they provide, job categories and salaries, etc.

Where Are the Overseas Jobs?

The Pacific Rim (South Korea, Hong Kong, Taiwan, Singapore, Thailand, Japan, and Indonesia), South America, Europe, Mexico, and Canada are all good countries to look for expatriate work. Major U.S.-based corporations (like Dell) have plants overseas and are always looking for qualified people. International airline companies have offices all around the world.

Hot Industries for Overseas Jobs
- Aerospace
- Entertainment (especially the film industry)
- Food and drink (companies like Coca-Cola, Pepsi, McDonald's, Burger King, etc).
- Petroleum (lots of jobs in China, Latin America and the Middle East)
- Telecommunications (jobs everywhere in this burgeoning field)

> For more information on international employment visit www.GlobalCareers.com, a global employment recruitment site and www.InternationalJobs.org, a membership-based site.

Job Opportunities Abroad by Category
- Executive/management/professional—senior managers, accountants, lawyers, doctors, engineers, geologists, economists, etc.
- Technical and service—translators, computer operators/programmers, administrative assistants, electricians, equipment operators, secretaries/word processors.
- Support positions—pipe fitters, welders, laborers, drivers, custodians/maintenance technicians, clerks, mechanics, carpenters, painters and plumbers.

Federal Agencies That Hire for Work Abroad
  1. The Department of State
     Foreign Service Recruitment Division
     P.O. Box 9317
     Rosslyn, VA 22209
     (202) 647-4000
     (Handles diplomatic relations with foreign governments)
  2. The Agency for International Development
     Recruitment Division (Promotes economic development abroad
     in more than 60 countries, including Africa)
     320 21st St. NW
     Washington, DC 20523
     (202) 663-1451
  3. International Trade Commission
     Personnel Division
     500 E. St. NW
     Washington, DC 20436
     (202) 205-2000
  4. Export-Import Bank
     Office of Personnel
     811 Vermont Ave., NW
     Washington, DC 20571
     (202) 566-8834

Tip: Don't forget to put your foreign language skills on your résumé.
This does not mean you can claim to speak Spanish if all you can say are
"enchilada" and "burrito."

For further information concerning travel abroad contact:
Superintendent of Government Documents
U. S. Government Printing Office
Washington, DC 20402
(202) 783-3263

Companies with a Conscience

"There are two ways of making money—one at the expense of others, the other by service to others. The first method does not "make" money, does not create anything; it only "gets" money—and does not always succeed in that."
—Henry Ford, 1928

Doing Good Works

For many people, just having a job with any company isn't fulfilling. Some people feel called to serve their communities by being part of a "socially-responsible" organization. Socially responsible companies have high standards with respect to how they run their businesses. These are companies that actively "give back" to their communities and are considered stewards of the environment. A social index is used to evaluate companies for social responsibility by measuring strengths in these areas: community, employee relations, the environment, women/minorities, products, military contracts, and use or support of nuclear power. According to *The Job Seeker's Guide to Socially Responsible Companies*, these companies are characterized by:

- trust and respect for individuals
- conducting business with integrity
- an emphasis on teamwork to achieve common objectives
- the encouragement of flexibility and innovation in a work environment that supports the diversity of people and ideas
- products and services of the highest quality and greatest possible value to the customer
- a commitment to help employees succeed by ensuring a safe and pleasant work environment, training and experience to help them gain a sense of satisfaction and accomplishment from their work, and providing the resources and benefits that make raising a family and pursuing a career compatible goals

- the recognition of obligations to being an economic and social asset to the communities

Ben & Jerry's, a Vermont-based ice cream company, has a longstanding reputation for being socially responsible by actively supporting local dairy farmers and treating workers as full partners in the company.

Get Paid to See the World

> *"To travel hopefully is a better thing than to arrive."*
> —Robert Louis Stevenson, novelist

Do you have an adventurous spirit? Have you ever wanted to live someplace really cool, maybe work outdoors and get paid for it? If so, then check out www.coolworks.com for jobs at Alaskan fishing lodges, on rivers (e.g. canoe guides), on lakes (like beautiful Lake Tahoe), at the beach, and at state and national parks. There are a lot of unconventional jobs out there in the wilderness.

Cruising the High Seas

> *"I travel not to go anywhere, but to go."*
> —Robert Louis Stevenson

The cruise line business is booming and new ships can't be built fast enough to satisfy the demand. Newer cruise ships, like small cities, sell luxury apartments to passengers who live on them for months at a time. Traversing the globe 365-days-a-year, these luxury leviathans offer fun, good food, and highly personalized service. Thousands of people are needed to staff these ships. Although some of the cruise ship jobs are skill intensive other jobs require little training. And because of the high employee turnover on these ships, there are always job openings.

How's the Pay?

Cruise ship workers can earn up to $3,000 per month or more, depending on the cruise line and the job.

A Cruise Ship Primer

A cruise ship's main areas are:

- Cruise Department—plans ship's activities and coordinates entertainment
- Purser's Department—accounting and administration
- Catering Department—prepares food for the entire ship
- Bar Department—"Cheers"
- Hotel Department—the second largest department on board
- Engine Department—engineers, electricians, plumbers, etc.
- Deck Department—responsible for ship's maintenance
- Service and Specialty Positions—beauty salon, photography, casino, etc.

Cruise ships are currently hiring in these areas:

- food and service
- entertainment/music
- deck/cabin stewards/stewardesses
- bartenders/cocktail servers
- retail/gift shops
- fitness/gym instructors
- youth counselors
- office personnel
- tour guides
- landside and reservationist positions
- medical staff
- casino dealers, and more

According to the cruise line industry increased terrorism has, to some degree, adversely affected the cruise line industry. In response to recent security concerns the cruise lines have adjusted their ports of call to avoid hot spots, and cruise ships are actually considered to be a very safe form of travel.

The Top Cruise Ship Employment Web Sites:

www.cruisejobline.com/—cruise ship jobs, information on the cruise industry and online applications forms

www.hcareers.com—thousands of jobs on cruise ships, in hotels, restaurants, casinos and resorts

www.cruiselinejobs.com—current cruise line jobs

www.cruiseshipjob.com—includes a complete listing of jobs, including "Urgent Vacancies" (these are often for positions as massage therapist, golf instructor, fitness instructor, and hair and nail technicians)

www.shipjobs.com—compiled by seasoned cruise ship worker Mark Landon, this site tells "the real truth about cruise ship jobs." Mr. Landon warns job hunters to beware of cruise line employment information that is for sale.

Cruise lines are very strict about the application process (there are a lot of forms to fill out) and will reject applications that are incorrect or incomplete. Follow the application instructions carefully.

Passport Please

You'll need a passport before being permitted to travel abroad. If you don't already have one, pick up an application at the post office, a court clerk's office, or at one of 13 passport agencies in larger U.S. cities. The U.S. Department of State's Bureau of Consulate Affairs at www.travel. state.gov/passport.services.html offers passport services. You must provide proof of your identity (like a birth certificate), two recent photos no larger than 2 x 2, and pay a $60 application fee.

If your passport has expired, you will need to fill out Form DS-82 and pay a $40 fee. It can take a few weeks to process your application, so if you need a passport in a hurry, you may pay an additional fee to rush processing or visit www.passportexpress.com (not a government agency) and get a passport in as little as 24 hours—their telephone number is 1-800-362-8196.

For medical questions about traveling abroad contact:
International Association for Medical Assistance to Travelers
417 Center Street
Lewiston, NY 14092
(716) 754-4883

Start Your Own Business

"If you haven't the strength to impose your own terms upon life then you must accept the terms it offers you."
—T. S. Eliot, poet, critic and playwright

Hundreds of thousands of Americans have started businesses. Unfortunately, many have failed due to inadequate planning and insufficient cash reserves. If you are considering starting a business, be prepared. There are considerable risks to starting your own business, not the least of which is failure. And there may be little income for the first few months. Some experts recommend that you have at least one year's worth of living funds set aside. The good news is that you don't have to reinvent the wheel since so many before you have been there.

The Business Plan

Start with a plan. A business plan is the blueprint for your business. It describes your mission, objectives, business model, financing, roles and responsibilities, long-term goals, the market, product or service, etc. Do not start your business without one. The Small Business Administration (more on the SBA in a bit) can help you, or you may purchase software with business plan templates ready to fill in with your information. After you write your business plan take it for evaluation to someone who has been in business. Try to find a mentor to advise you throughout the start-up process.

How to Succeed in Business without Being White

"People are always blaming their circumstances for what they are. I don't believe in circumstances. The people who get on in this world are the people who get up and look for the circumstances they want, and if they can't find them, make them."
—George Bernard Shaw, dramatist and literary critic

There are approximately 900,000 black-owned businesses in the United States today with the top 100 black businesses boasting annual sales of more than $12 billion. According to the U.S. Department of Commerce, Bureau of the Census, the number of businesses owned by African-Americans in the United States increased almost 50 percent during the 1990s.

The District of Columbia had the largest percentage of African-American-owned firms, followed by Maryland and Mississippi. These figures are not surprising considering that blacks account for almost two-thirds of the population in the District of Columbia and one-fourth of the population in Maryland.

Starting a business is a dream for many people, but for African-Americans there are often cultural hurdles to jump. Many blacks fear that if they try to penetrate the corporate world that they must assimilate into the white business culture. Earl Graves, successful black businessman and author, says this is true to some extent. Graves admits there are certain behaviors necessary for participating in the business world (like wearing a suit or learning to play golf) but he believes that most successful blacks in the business world have not forgotten who they are or where they came from. For further information on minority-owned businesses, contact the Census Bureau's Minority-and Women-owned Businesses Information Staff at 301-763-5726.

Mark Henricks's new book, *Not Just a Living: the Complete Guide to Creating a Business That Gives You a Life*, outlines a process for helping people assess their potential for going into business for themselves.

> Visit www.LittleAfrica.com/financial/ for advice on financial
> and wealth-building strategies for African-Americans. Little-
> Africa.com also has informative articles covering a wide range
> of topics including savings, financial planning, taxes, investing
> and estate planning.

Black Business Network

Networking, the importance of which has been emphasized
throughout this book, is absolutely crucial when trying to break into
the business world. People running their own businesses must network
within their industry, with customers, bankers, lawyers, local politicians, and community groups. The more people you know, the more
business you will attract and the better informed you will be about the
market. Walk up to someone at a professional meeting and introduce
yourself. Ask them what they do and often they will ask you what you
do. This is the time for your "elevator speech."

Free Help

Fortunately, there are resources to help you start your own business.
The Small Business Administration (SBA) was created by Congress in
1953 to help entrepreneurs form successful small enterprises. There are
currently around 20 million small businesses that create two out of
every three jobs in the United States. Go to the SBA Web site at
www.sba.gov/ and request a business "Start-up Kit." The SBA also provides counseling services, workshops, help writing business plans, and
information on patents, trademarks, and financing.

Historically Underutilized Business (HUB)

In some states, including North Carolina, Ohio and Texas, African-
American entrepreneurs, suppliers, and vendors, etc. may be eligible to
form a Historically Underutilized Business (HUB). Kind of like
affirmative action for businesses, various state agencies and universities,

like the University of Houston's, define a HUB as: "a corporation formed for the purpose of making a profit in which at least 51% of all shares or other securities are owned by one or more persons who are socially disadvantaged…members of certain groups, including Black Americans, Hispanics, women, Asian Americans and Native Americans, and have suffered the effects of discriminatory practices or similar insidious circumstances over which they have no control." (Source: University of Houston's Web site, www.uh.edu/mapp/04/040108.htm).

The HUB program was established to aid minority business owners who had previously been excluded from participating in the mainstream business world. To get HUB certification you must fill out an application with the General Service Commission of the state in which you want to do business. The State of Texas mandates that thirty percent of contracts, supplies, materials, services and equipment purchased for the state be awarded to HUBs. It is clear there are enormous opportunities here for blacks.

Franchising

Recently, large, well-known franchises like Motel 6, Dunkin' Donuts, KFC, and Long John Silver's, have begun to actively recruit women and minorities. Franchising offers several advantages over starting a business from scratch, not the least of which are marketing support, specialized training, and ready-made business plans. These advantages are particularly attractive to people who do not have a family history of business ownership or access to investment capital.

Women now account for about one-third of all franchise business owners and franchise opportunities for minorities have never been stronger. "The inner cities are largely untapped markets," says Robert Bond, founder of the National Minority Franchising Initiative (www.minorityfranchising.com). The NMFI seeks to "empower minorities and bring business ownership opportunities within their reach." If you have ever dreamed of owning your own business, consider a franchise.

Not-for-Profit

Organizations whose primary missions are to serve their communities rather than just make money are known as non-profit or not-for-profit. The Internal Revenue Service exempts these entities from federal taxes. Well-known not-for-profits include Planned Parenthood, the American Civil Liberties Union (ACLU), and the National Organization for the Advancement of Colored People (NAACP). Although salaries are generally lower than in the private sector, people who work for these agencies are usually there to do good works and serve others. Many people find working in these organizations to be less stressful than in a strictly money-making environment. Others find that on-the-job training and experience more than make up for the lower pay. Most not-for-profit agencies provide benefits like health insurance and paid vacations for full-time workers. To find a job in a non-profit setting visit www.nonprofitjobs.org, a site "dedicated to those who serve others."

Volunteer Opportunities

"The only gift is a portion of thyself."
—Ralph Waldo Emerson, essayist and poet

You may be thinking about going into a particular line of work but have little experience in the field. To correct this, consider volunteer work that allows you to get the experience you need. Many cities have Volunteer Centers that are clearinghouses for organizations who recruit volunteers. You may also contact any company, hospital, or service industry and offer to do volunteer work for them. Try not to commit to more than one day a week so you can continue looking for a "real" job. Benefits to volunteering include:

- getting an insider's view of the business/organization
- learning new skills
- real work experience for your résumé
- good references

5,000 a Day

If you can't think of an organization for which you would like to volunteer, visit www.volunteermatch.org to get some ideas. Just type in your zip code, how far you're willing to travel, when you're available and your interests, and you'll be matched with one of the 20,450 groups nationwide that use this free service to find volunteers. Five thousand potential volunteers sign up at this site every day. A site where you can make a donation to charity or select a cause for which to volunteer is www.networkforgood.com. Volunteer opportunities can be found in areas such as animals and the environment, health, religion, arts and culture, or human services.

In whatever path you choose, make your ethnic background work for you. There has never been a better time to be a black job hunter.

See Recommended Reading for further information on this chapter's contents.

CHAPTER 8

"Tell Me about Yourself"

Although dreaded by many job hunters, the interview may well be the most important step to getting a job. This chapter will help you prepare for commonly asked questions, quickly discern what is and what is not working during the interview, negotiate salary, interview the interviewer, and have the confidence to perform your absolute best.

"The greatest thing in this world is not so much where we stand as in what direction we are moving."
—Oliver Wendell Holmes, Jr., Assoc. Justice of the Supreme Court (1902-32)

Attitude is Everything

"Attitude determines altitude"
—Anonymous

An interview is an opportunity to sell your self. Although communicating your skills, abilities and achievements during the interview is a big factor in securing a position, an employer is also interested in **who** you are. The key element to successful interviewing is not your experience or grade point average, but your **attitude**. Your attitude determines whether you are in or out. Employers are looking for individuals who can become "family" and contribute to the organization's growth.

Know the Organization

A successful interview begins with preparation. Learn something about the company before the interview to demonstrate interest. The best way to research a company and its interview process is by knowing someone inside the organization. This person can tell you about the company's goals and possibly about the person who will be interviewing you. If you don't know anyone who works for the organization, read the company's Annual Report, especially the "President's Letter to Shareholders." This will tell you about the company's mission, goals, and accomplishments, and you will come across like an insider during the interview.

Anticipate Questions

Before the interview, review and memorize your skills and work-related characteristics. Think of real examples to demonstrate how your skills were used. Anticipate questions about information on your résumé (see section on interview questions), and be prepared to talk about strengths and weaknesses.

Before you go to the actual interview do a mock interview with friends or family to practice.

The Interview Process

"I don't think in terms of failure. I don't feel like anyone outside of me should be setting limitations. People should shoot for the moon."
—Whoopi Goldberg, actress

OK, you're on!

The interview is like an audition or a performance. If you haven't rehearsed, then don't be surprised if you flub the interview. If **you** don't impress the interviewer, the next applicant will. Consider what the interviewer wants to know. Keep in mind that you represent a financial risk to the employer if you turn out to be a hiring mistake.

As the interview begins, let the employer set the stage and then follow their lead. Tone of voice and overall pace are good cues. Pay attention to the little things they say that you can use to build rapport. If you've been able to find out something in advance about the person interviewing, then use that knowledge now.

Your two main goals in an interview are:
1. To convince the interviewer that you're the right person for the job
2. To learn more about the job and the organization.

Nearly every employer is looking for:
- a positive attitude toward work
- proficiency in field
- communication skills (oral and written)
- interpersonal skills
- confidence
- critical thinking and problem solving skills
- flexibility
- self-motivation
- growth potential
- leadership
- teamwork

Look Professional

Always dress conservatively to interviews. No jeans or sweatshirts with sports team logos. Business suits for men and women are preferred or longer (over-the knee) skirts and tasteful blouses for women. And don't forget the shoes. Some people (especially ex-military) form an impression based on the appearance of shoes. Make sure yours are clean and polished. Never chew gum or light up a cigarette in an interview.

Check-in

Be on time. In fact, arrive a few minutes early. Your first personal contact with the company may be with the receptionist or secretary. Make friends with them because interviewers often ask them about their impressions of you after you've left. And when you call later, the receptionist is more likely to remember you and put the call through.

Nervous Jitters

The curtain is about to rise and you've suddenly got stage fright. Hopefully, you've practiced interviewing and are prepared. Here's how to calm your body. Breathe in deeply through your nose, then contract your abdominal muscles and slowly exhale through your lips. Hold it at the bottom, take in another deep breath, and you're all set. If you get nervous during the interview, simply pause, take a deep breath, exhale and contract and continue. Don't forget that the interviewer might be nervous too.

Body Language

> *"What you say is not nearly as important as how you say it."*
> —Annette Segall, career management consultant

Research suggests that nonverbal communication like body language is more important in understanding someone than in what they actually say. Your body language is how you communicate through facial expressions, posture, gestures and movements, etc., that reveal what you are really thinking. Most people are unconscious of their body language. Have someone evaluate yours using this guide.

Eye contact—Maintaining good eye contact during the interview may be the most important nonverbal communication you make. If you look away while speaking, it shows either a lack of confidence or that you're lying.

Facial expressions—Try to smile and act like you're delighted to be there. This doesn't mean you have to look goofy, but a warm smile works wonders. Make the time pleasant for the interviewer.

Posture—To send a signal of confidence and power, stand and walk tall, and when seated, sit at the edge of the chair leaning slightly forward.

Gestures—Don't overuse

Here are some body language characteristics to keep in mind:

Openness and warmth are characterized by open-lipped smiling and open hands with palms visible.

Confidence is displayed by leaning forward in chair, chin up, putting tips of fingers of one hand against the tips of fingers in "praying" positions, and hands joined behind back when standing.

Nervousness manifests as smoking, whistling, pinching skin, fidgeting, jiggling pocket contents, clearing throat, twiddling thumbs, biting fingernails, wringing hands, and biting on pens.

Untrustworthy/defensive body language include frowning, squinting eyes, tight-lipped grin, arms crossed in front of chest, chin down, darting eyes, looking down when speaking, clenched hands, chopping one hand into the open palm of the other, rubbing back of neck. (Source: Fast, Julius, *Body Language*, Pocket Books, 1970).

Critical Factors in an Interview

The intent of the interview is to get a second interview or a job offer. There are three steps to the interview process. You must complete each step before proceeding.

1. **Establish rapport**—Greet the interviewer with a medium grip handshake and mirror the handshake being offered. Most professional people are turned off by a limp handshake. The establishing rapport step is where first impressions are formed. Research indi-

cates that many employers make a decision about a candidate in 15 to 20 seconds. If you start the interview off poorly it will be difficult to regain ground. *Personal appearance* is the first thing the interviewer notices. *How you speak* during the interview and *your ability to articulate your background* will earn you high marks. No matter how good your résumé or how well you answer the questions, you won't get the job unless you *make a personal connection* with the interviewer. People hire those they are comfortable with.

2. **Gather information**—In this step the employer will ask questions and try to match your answers to the company's needs. These are questions about your background and to reveal your attitude and work ethic. You will also learn about the company with which you are interviewing.

3. **Close**—If you have succeeded in selling yourself up to this point, the interviewer will try to sell you on the company and discuss the next step. If you were not successful, the conversation will likely turn to the movies or the weather, etc.

Tip: Don't forget to bring extra copies of your résumé to the interview and a pad with which to take notes.

Typical Questions Employers Ask

Before you convince the interviewer you're right for the job, you have to believe it yourself. Try to answer questions in ways that relate to job performance, quality of your work, safety, and your desire to be a team player. Be confident.

Some of these questions will likely be asked during your interview. Prepare your own responses. (I've included some sample answers).

Q: Describe your short-range and long-range goals.

A: Short-range goals are to get this job and learn new skills, and the long-range ones are to make a meaningful contribution to this organization and its continued success and move higher within the organization.

Q: Why are you leaving your present position?

A: It is time for new challenges and I know this is the organization where I can find them.

Q: What can you do for us that someone else cannot do?

A: I can bring in an entirely new customer base.

Q: Why should we hire you?

A: No other candidate has my skills and experience. Additionally, my outgoing personality and commitment to excellence are what you're looking for.

Q: Why do you want to work here?

A: This company's reputation for being the best is widely known and I only work for the best. Your mission is something I strongly support.

Q: What was your worst job?

A: There are good and bad things about every job. (Never badmouth a previous employer or you'll sound like you're not a team player. Say that you learned certain skills on your last job or that you solved a particular problem).

Q: What kind of salary are you worth?

A: I'm sure we can come to an agreement about compensation when an offer is extended.

Q: What are your five biggest accomplishments in your present or last job?

A: You should have these memorized—list them.

Q: How long would you stay with us if we hire you?

A: I am looking for a career in this field and would hope to make a contribution for many years.

Q: What is your biggest strength? Weakness?

A: The strength part is easy; convert your weakness into a positive. You could say that although you used to have a problem with multi-tasking, your last supervisor helped you learn to do it right. You also learned it's OK to ask for help.

Q: How do you define success?

A: How do **they** define success?

Q: How would you describe your personality?

A: Tell them.

Q: How would you handle racist comments or jokes at work?

A: What are the company policies regarding this type of speech? Hopefully, this would not be tolerated in your organization. No one should suffer indignities like that, especially in the workplace.

Q: Have you ever supervised people? Hired or fired people?

A: Tell them if you have.

Q: Where do you see yourself in five years?

A: Talk about **this** position and how you will meet the company's needs. Tell them you hope there will be many opportunities for professional growth within this organization.

Q: Tell me about yourself.

A: Tailor your answer to match the employer's needs. Toot your own horn.

Q: What other companies are you interviewing with?

A: Be truthful about other interested employers.

Q: Is there anything else I need to know about you?

A: Last chance to close the sale.

For more tips on improving your interviewing technique visit these Web sites:

- www.quintcareers.com/interview_questions.html—lists 50 common questions to expect in an interview
- www.wetfeet.com/advice/interviewing.asp—insights by experts into the interviewing process.

> **The Five Categories of Questions in an Interview**
> **Credential:** Tell me about your certification in XYZ programming language.
> **Experience:** Do you know how to operate a sticky widget?
> **Opinion:** Is it ever OK to "borrow" supplies from the company to take home? (No!).
> **Dumb:** If you were an animal, what kind of animal would you be?
> **Behavioral:** Can you tell me how you would handle a rude customer? ("I would be courteous, recognize they are upset, try to identify the problem and offer solutions that meet everyone's needs.").

The Parrot Technique

If you are asked a question that throws you off or for which you are unprepared and you need a moment to compose yourself, you can stall the interviewer by parroting the question. "If I understand you correctly, you're asking _____." Another stalling device is, "Can you tell me exactly how this plays a role in the company?"

What If They Ask an Illegal Question?

You feel like the interview is going well and then out of the blue you hear, "Your people place a high value on that, don't they?" Or, "Are you considering having children?" These questions may seem innocent, but they are improper in a formal interview. It doesn't necessarily mean, however, a crime has been committed. Most illegal questions are asked in ignorance, not with malicious intent.

Depending on the state where asked, the following questions may be illegal, and viewed as an intention to discriminate:

- Questions about birthplace, nationality, ancestry, or descent of applicant: "Ricardo—is that a Spanish name?"
- Questions related to applicant's sex or marital status: "Is that your maiden name?"

- Questions related to race or color: "Are you considered to be part of a minority group?"
- Questions related to religion or religious holidays observed: "Does your religion prevent you from working weekends or holidays?"
- Questions related to physical disabilities or handicaps: "Do you need special glasses for this job?"
- Questions related to health or medical history: "Do you have any pre-existing health conditions?"
- Questions related to pregnancy, birth control, and childcare: "Are you planning on having children?" (this line of prohibited questioning was added in a 1978 amendment to the Civil Rights Act).

(Source: www.eeoc.gov)

How Should You Respond?

What is the proper response to possibly illegal or, at the very least, offensive questions? Unless the question is blatantly discriminatory, your best move is to change the subject. If, however, the question is too offensive, you have the right to end the interview and leave. Whether you report the incident (and, other than your testimony, what proof do you have this question was asked?) is up to you. You can always file a formal report with appropriate federal agencies (See Chapter 6) if you think one is warranted. Consider spreading the word about this company at black Web sites and throughout your network.

Interview the Interviewer

Now the interviewer asks, "Do you have any questions?" You answer, "Yes."

Questions to ask the interviewer (if they haven't already been answered):

- What is the most important part of this job?
- Is there a problem in your company that needs immediate attention?
- Is this a new position or am I replacing someone?
- Why has this job become available?

- Could you describe my responsibilities—may I see a copy of the job description?
- To whom will I be reporting?
- Why did you decide to work for this company?
- Does this company offer training?
- Are performance reviews given and, if so, how often?
- Do you promote from within when a position becomes available?
- What characteristics do your best employees have in common?
- What opportunities are there for advancement in this company?
- When will you make your selection?

Exams and Testing

If you are asked to take an exam or test it could be a good sign because employers don't usually waste their time with someone they're not interested in.

1. The five kinds of pre-employment tests are:
2. Intelligence/mental ability
3. Work simulation
4. Specific skills test
5. Personality test— would you rather fly a kite or read a novel?
6. Honesty test— usually for high security jobs or those with access to cash

Be sure you fully understand the test's instructions before you begin. Occasionally, an organization might even analyze your handwriting (graphology) to assess personality characteristics.

Ask for the Job

At the end of the interview recap why you feel you are the best candidate and restate your interest in the position by asking for the job.

"I like what I have seen and heard today and I want to work for you. When may I start?"

Don't bring up money too quickly in the first interview. If asked early in the interview what salary you expect, indicate what your current/last salary is/was and leave it at that. There will be time to negotiate salary and benefits later.

Negotiating Offers

"Experience is not what happens to you. It is what you do with what happens to you."
—Aldous Huxley, novelist and critic

Negotiating is what you do after an offer is made. Create a favorable impression by speaking up for yourself in negotiating for a higher salary. If you've stressed your accomplishments during the interview and demonstrated your understanding of the company and its problems and goals, you'll come across as a serious committed player. This is what employers are looking for.

Negotiating the Terms

Salary is often the primary issue in negotiation. First get the offer then negotiate. If you have a true job offer, the first thing you need to do is decide if it's acceptable in its present form. If you still have unanswered questions about the position, ask them now.

The Range

To establish a salary range for the position, ask, "What is the salary range for new hires in this position?" Or, "What would a person with my background and qualifications typically earn in this position?" Then, "Do you ever pay higher than that range? If so, for what reason?" And, "Of course, money is only one element and I will be evaluating the whole package." Don't be too specific when the interviewer tries to pin down your salary requirements.

Interview Report Card: How did you do?

Analyze your performance. Think of what was said during the interview. Were your responses to difficult questions good? Did you address the interviewer's concerns? What questions did you have trouble answering and what needs improving?

Your interview went well and an offer may be pending if:

· You are introduced to other employees in the office
· You are given a tour of the facility
· You are given information about the local area
· You are given an employee handbook
· You are introduced to the big boss

Accepting/Rejecting the Offer

If the salary range is acceptable say, "That would be acceptable, depending on the whole salary and benefits package." If the range is below your expectations you could say, "The other companies I am currently speaking with are considering me at a salary somewhat higher than that range." (Be careful, though, if this is a weak negotiating card). Always say you were "hoping" for more, instead of "expecting" more.

If you feel the offer is unacceptable, you must determine what will make it acceptable. It's not always just money. These areas are often negotiable:

· Salary
· Bonuses
· Profit sharing
· Stock options
· Benefits
· Training
· Overtime
· Other (company car, travel reimbursement, etc.)

If the offer is still unacceptable, say so while maintaining a positive outlook for resolution:

"I am still very interested in working with you and your company. However, at this point I am not able to accept the offer for the following reason: (state your reason and what part of the offer is missing). If you were able to _____ (give a proposed solution), I would gladly accept the position immediately. Are you in a position to help?" Depending on the interviewer's power to make concessions, you may get everything you want. But you also run the risk of having the deal fall through if your terms can't be met.

If you are comfortable with closing this sale, you can add, "Are you ready to make me an offer?" A sense of urgency can help them move quickly if they want you.

Salary Comparison Calculator

If you accept an offer in another city and want the true value of the offer, you can survey salaries in any city you choose. This salary survey Web site can help you compare salaries and cost of living averages in over 100 cities throughout the U.S.: www.homefair. com/homefair/cmr/salcalc.html. Select the base city then enter a salary and a target city. The salary calculator will respond with the comparable salary in the target city. Other sites that offering salary comparisons are www.jobstar.org/tools/salary/sal-surv.htm and www.3.fu.com/acinet/.

Follow-up

"Perseverance is a great element of success…if you only knock long enough and loud enough at the gate, you are sure to wake up somebody."
—George Bernard Shaw

After the interview be sure to call the interviewer to thank him or her for their time and write a short note reemphasizing interest in the position. If you need to clarify or add something, this is the time to do it.

Stay in contact with the interviewer by calling once a week to say you're still interested and ask what the next step is.

You're Hired!

The Big Announcement

This is the moment you have worked for. An offer has been extended and you are pleased with most, if not all of the entire package. Give yourself credit where credit is due. You created a plan, laid out goals, identified resources, talked to a lot of people, surfed the Net, registered with job-finding Web sites, lined up interviews, put on a necktie or pantyhose, survived grueling interviews, and were eventually rewarded for all your efforts.

Don't forget to send a thank you note to everyone in your network who helped you along the way. And for those who did a little extra to help you get the job, send a small gift and a personal note of thanks. They will remember the gesture.

A New Routine

"The man who goes farthest is generally the one who is willing to do and dare. The "sure-thing" boat never gets far from the shore."
—Dale Carnegie, motivational coach and author

Naturally, you will want to shine in the first days at your new job. Pay attention to what is said and done so you can quickly learn about the company and what is expected of you. To start off on the right foot:

- Be on time
- Study the people who are successful in the company and emulate them
- Greet others in the morning with a smile
- Don't use profanity or tell off-color jokes
- Develop a reputation as a problem-solver
- Never discuss your salary with co-workers
- Don't gossip
- Learn to become a team player

Conclusion

Most interviews last about five minutes even if the "real" interview lasts half an hour. If you haven't convinced the interviewer you're the right person for the job by then, it's going to be tough. In the first five minutes the employer notes your appearance, grooming, handshake, eye contact, articulation, and personality. You must stand out from the competition.

What characterizes success at work? Successful people have a need to be the best at whatever they do. Are you ready for success? If you believe in yourself, the rest will follow. Good luck in your job search. Your dream career awaits you.

"No matter how long the night, the day is sure to come."
—African Proverb

Recommended Reading

The Adventure of Working Abroad, by Joyce Sautters Osland, Jossey-Bass, 1995, ISBN: 0787901083. All types of testimonials of individuals who have worked abroad.

American Jobs Abroad, By Victoria Harlow and Edward Knappman, New England Publishing Associates, 1994, ISBN: 0810388995. Although a bit expensive ($92.50), this book has everything you need to find overseas employment. It lists over 800 companies that offer jobs abroad. You can browse the index of job categories to narrow your company list to those with opportunities in your field.

Breaking the Glass Ceiling, by Anthony Stith, Warwick Publishing, 1998, ISBN: 1-894020-20-0. Black business editor Stith discusses racism and sexism in corporate America and remedies for same.

CareerXRoads 2002, The Directory to Job, Résumé and Career Management Sites on the Web, by Gerry Crispin and Mark Mehler, MMC Group, 2002, ISBN: 0-9652239-0-6 (section on diversity).

The Complete Idiot's Guide to the Perfect Job Interview, by Marc A. Dorio, Macmillan General Reference, 1997, ISBN: 0028619455. This book provides tips for handling all kinds of interviews, how to answer tricky questions, tips for negotiating salary, how to dress, and how to overcome objections.

Directory of Special Programs for Minority Group Members: Career Information Services, Employment Skills Banks, Financial Aid Sources, Willis L. Johnson's, 4th ed. Garrett Park Press, P.O. Box 190, Garrett

Park, MD 20896. Information about programs that benefit minority applicants.

Guide to Internet Job Searching, 2002-03, Dikel, Margaret and Roehm, Francis, VGM Career Books, 2002, ISGN: 0-07-138310-7.

How to Succeed in Business without Being White, by Earl Graves, Harper Business, 1997, ISBN: 0-88730-808-02. Publisher and CEO of Black Enterprises, Graves is a nationally recognized authority on black business development. This book has great advice for minorities entering the job market for the first time, trying to break into corporate America, or starting a business.

Internet Résumés, by Peter D. Weddle, Impact Publications, 1998, ISBN: 1-57023-094-3. Tells you how to create and post résumés on the Web.

Job Power: The Young People's Job Finding Guide, by Haldane, Bernard, and Jean, and Martin, Lowell, Acropolis Books Ltd., 2400 17th St. NW, Washington, DC 20009

The Job Seeker's Guide to Socially Responsible Companies, by Katherine Janowski, Visible Ink Press, 1995, ISBN: 0810322943. This guide was written for job seekers that want to work for a socially responsible company. Research has shown that these types of companies have higher employee loyalty and commitment and attract the best employees. Contains an alphabetical listing of 1,000 American companies.

Not Just a Living: The Complete Guide to Creating a Business That Gives You a Life, by Mark Henricks. This book advocates the concept of "lifestyle entrepreneur," people who live where they want, do the work they want to do, and do it with people they like. It will help you build a personally and professionally rewarding business.

The Résumé Handbook: How to Write Outstanding Résumés and Cover Letters for Every Situation, by Arthur D. Roesenberg, David V. Hizer, Adams Media Corporation, ISBN: 1558506160, 3rd edition, June 1996.

Unofficial Guide to Hot Careers, by Shelly Field, MacMillan 2000, ISBN: 0-02-863416-0. Latest career news and assistance in developing a good job-hunting plan.

We Want Jobs: A History of Affirmative Action, by Robert Weiss, Garland Publishing, Inc., 1997, ISBN: 0-8153-2750-1 ($75.00). A good history of the struggle by minorities for equal employment opportunities from slavery times to today.

What Color is Your Parachute?, by Richard Nelson Bolles, Ten Speed Press, 1999, ISBN: 1580081258

Internet Resources

Black-focused Web Sites

www.bcw.org—Black Career Women

www.naacp.org—NAACP's Home Page

www.nul.org—National Urban League

www.naacpjobfair.com—NAACP's job fair site

www.ntu.edu.sg/home/ctng/assoc.htm—professional black associations

www.bdpa.org—Black Data Processor Associates; links to local chapters

www.BlackEnterprise.com—"The virtual desktop for African-Americans"

www.blackeoejournal.com—Black Equal Opportunity Employment Journal Magazine

www.BlackWeb.net—news, culture, networking, employment

www.BlackVoices.com—780,000 members; career center

www.Blinks.net—technology-oriented; career center

www.diversitycareers.com—careers in engineering and information technology

www.DiversityInc.com—excellent comprehensive site with career center

www.Diversityemployment.com—multicultural employment resources

www.Diversitylink.com/index.htm—bringing together diversity professionals

www.diversityrecruiting.com/index2.html—leads diversity candidates to some of America's best companies

www.diversitysearch.com/index2.html—a woman-owned site, "helping to promote diversity in the workplace"

www.eop.com—Equal Opportunity Publications, Inc.

www.EverythingBlack.com—business, culture, education, etc.

www.HireDiversity.com—employment resources for minorities

www.IMDiversity.com—search jobs, post résumés, check employer profiles

www.minority-professionalnetwork.com—choose desired metropolitan area

www.netnoir.com—the black network

www.nsbe.org/—National Society of Black Engineers

www.ReadingBlack.com—literary news, calendar of events, and a jobs section

www.TBWT.com—Black World Today—offers free résumé hosting

www.iminorities.com—"Where careers, opportunity and diversity connect"

www.aawc.com/aap.html—African American publications

Black Periodicals

www.Ebony.com

www.Essence.com

www.Jet.com

www.Black-Collegian.com

Career and Employment Resources (descriptions in Chapter 3)

www.allretailjobs.com

www.ajb.dni.us

www.bestjobsusa.com

www.careerbabe.com

www.careerbuilder.com

www.careercenter.net

www.careercity.com

www.careerjournal.com

www.careermosaic.com

www.careerpath.com

www.careershop.com
www.careertips.com
www.citysearch.com
www.employmentguide.com
www.employmentspot.com
www.flipdog.com
www.Headhunter.net
www.hire.com
www.hotjobs.com
www.hotresumes.com
www.joboptions.com
www.hightechcareers.com
www.job.com
www.jobs.com
www.jobsonline.com
www.kaplancareers.com
www.monster.com
www.rileyguide.com
www.wetfeet.com
www.workzone.net
www.yahoo.com

College Graduates

www.asktheheadhunter.com
www.campuscareercenter.com
www.collegegrad.com
www.jobtrak.com
www.truecareers.com

Chat Sites

www.chatlist.com
www.cnn.com

www.groups.yahoo.com
www.msnbc.com
www.talkcity.com

Company Information
www.fortune.com/lists/diversity/index.html
http://business.lycos.com/companyresearch/crtop.asp

Federal Government Employment Resources
www.usajobs.opm.gov
www.fbi.gov
www.fbijobs.com
www.fedworld.gov
www.ins.usdoj.gov
www.tsa.dot.gov/employment_opps/securityscreeners_index.shtm
www.tsa.gov/contacts/contact_us.shtm
www.usdoj.gov
www.usajobs.opm.gov

Small Business Administration
www.sba.gov/

Educators Resources
www.teachersplanet.com

Aerobics and Fitness Association of America
www.aerobics.com

Bilingual Professionals
www.bilingual-jobs.com
www.Brint.com

Chef's Resources
www.uspca.com

www.greatchefs.com
www.starchefs.com

Court Reporters

www.verbatimreporters.com
www.certmag.com

Emergency Medical Technician

www.angelfire.com/ok/marvin1226—EMT Chad Moser's site

E-Learning Web Sites

www.bn.com
www.capella.edu
www.classesusa.com
www.click2learn.com
www.ecollege.com
www.encarta.msn.com/elearning
www.fathom.com
www.horizonlive.com
www.learnittoday.com
www.learnkey.com
www.learn2.com
www.primelearning.com
www.smartforce.com/
www.trainingserver.com

Employment Discrimination

www.eeoc.gov

Drug Testing

www.collegegrad.com
www.preemploymentdrugtests.com

Outdoor and Nontraditional Jobs
www.coolworks.com

International Employment
www.GlobalCareers.com
www.InternationalJobs.org

Passport Services
www.travel.state.gov/passport.services.html
www.passportexpress.com

Cruise Ship Jobs
www.cruisejobline.com/
www.hcareers.com
www.cruiselinejobs.com
www.cruiseshipjob.com
www.shipjobs.com

Non-profit and Volunteer Resources
www.networkforgood.com
www.nonprofitjobs.org
www.volunteermatch.org

Salary Survey Sites for Different Cities
www.homefair.com/homefair/cmr/salcalc.html
www.jobstar.org/tools/salary/sal-surv.htm
www.3.fu.com/acinet/.

Search Engines
www.ask.com
www.google.com
www.hotbot.com
www.altavista.com

www.metacrawler.com
www.expertcentral.com
www.nytimes.com/library/tech/reference/cynavi.html
www.invisibleweb.com/
www.completeplanet.com/
www.webdata.com/

Web Development

www.sitepoint.com

State Employment Service Offices

ALABAMA Employment Service, Dept. of Industrial Relations, 469 Monroe Street, Montgomery, AL 36130, (334) 242-8990

ALASKA Employment Service Department of Labor, P.O. Box 25509, Juneau, AK 99802-5509, (907) 4652712

ARIZONA Department of Economic Security, P.O. Box 6123-010A, Phoenix, AZ 85005, (602) 542-5678

ARKANSAS Employment Security Division, P.O. Box 2981, Little Rock, AR 72203, (501) 682-2121

CALIFORNIA Job Service Division, P.O. Box 826880-MIG 37, Sacramento, CA 94280-0001, (916) 654-9047

COLORADO Department of Labor & Employment, 1515 Arapaho St., Tower 2, Suite 400, Denver, CO 80202-2117, (303) 620-4700

CONNECTICUT Labor Department, 200 Folly Brook Blvd., Wethersfield, CT 06109, (860) 566-4384

DELAWARE Department of Labor, 820 North French St., 6th Fl., Wilmington, DE 19714-9499, (302) 577-2713

DISTRICT OF COLUMBIA Department of Employment Services, 500 C Street, NW, Rm. 600, Washington, D.C. 20001, (202) 724-7107

FLORIDA Department of Labor & Employment Security, 2012 Capitol Circle, SE, Suite 303, Hartman Bldg., Tallahassee, FL 32399-2152, (904) 922-7021

GEORGIA Department of Labor, 148 International Blvd., NE, Suite 400, Atlanta, GA 30303, (404) 656-3011

HAWAII Department of Labor & Industrial Relations, 830 Punchbowl St., Room 320, Honolulu HI 96813, (808) 586-8844

IDAHO Department of Employment, 317 Main Street, Boise, ID 83735, (208) 334-6110

ILLINOIS Department of Employment Security, 401 South State St., Suite 624, Chicago, IL 60605, (312) 793-9279

INDIANA Department of Workforce Development, 10 North Senate Avenue, Indianapolis, IN 46204-2277, (317) 233-5661

IOWA Department of Employment Services, 1000 East Grand Avenue, Des Moines, IA 50309, (515) 281-5365

KANSAS Department of Human Resources, 401 Topeka Blvd., Topeka, KS 66603, (913) 296-7474

KENTUCKY Department for Employment Services, 275 E. Main Street, Frankfort, KY 40621, (502) 564-5331

LOUISIANA Office of Employment Security, P.O. Box 94094, Baton Rouge, LA 70804-9094, (504) 342-3013

MAINE Department of Labor, P.O. Box 309, Augusta, ME 0433-0309, (207) 287-3788

MARYLAND Department of Economic & Employment Development, 1100 North Eutaw St., Rm. 600, Baltimore, MD 21201, (410) 767-2400

MASSACHUSETTS Department of Employment & Training, 19 Stanford St., 3rd Floor, Boston, MA 02114, (617) 626-6600

MICHIGAN Employment Security Commission, 7310 Woodward Avenue, Detroit, MI 48202, (313) 876-5901

MINNESOTA Department of Economic Security, 390 North Robert St., St. Pau, MN 55101, (612) 296-3711

MISSISSIPPI Employment Security Commission, P.O. Box 1699, Jackson, MS 39215-1699, (601) 961-7400

MISSOURI Department of Labor and Industrial Relations, P.O. Box 504, Jefferson City, MO 65102-0505, (314) 751-4091

MONTANA Department of Labor & Industry, State Capitol, Helena, MT 59624, (406) 444-3555

NEBRASKA Department of Labor, 550 South 15th St., Lincoln, NE 68509 (402) 471-3405

NEVADA Department of Employment Training and Rehabilitation, 1830 East Sahara, Las Vegas, NV 89104 (702) 486-7923

NEW HAMPSHIRE Department of Employment Security, 32 South Main Street, Concord, NH 03301-4857

NEW JERSEY Department of Labor CN, 110 Trenton, NJ 08625-011, (609) 292-2323

NEW MEXICO Department of Labor, P.O. Box 1928, Albuquerque, NM 87103, (305) 841-8409

NEW YORK Department of Labor, State Campus Building 12, Albany, NY 12240, (518) 457-2741

NORTH CAROLINA Employment Security Commission, P.O. Box 25903, Raleigh, NC 27611, (919) 733-7546

NORTH DAKOTA Job Service ND, P.O. Box 5507, Bismarck, ND 58506-5507, (701) 328-2836

OHIO Bureau of Employment Services, 145 S. Front Street, Columbus, OH 43215, (614) 466-2100

OKLAHOMA Employment Security Commission, 215 Will Rogers Memorial Office Bldg., 2401 N. Lincoln, Oklahoma City, OK 73105, (405) 557-7201

OREGON Employment Department, 875 Union Street, N.E., Salem, OR 97311, (503) 378-3208

PENNSYLVANIA Department of Labor and Industry, Labor & Industry Building, Room 1700, Harrisburg, PA 17121, (717) 787-3756

PUERTO RICO Bureau of Employment Security, 505 Munoz Rivera Avenue, Hate Rey, PR 00918, (809) 754-5376

RHODE ISLAND Department of Employment and Training, 101 Friendship Street, Providence, RI 02903-3740, (401) 277-3732

SOUTH CAROLINA Employment Security Commission, P.O. Box 995, Columbia, SC 29202, (803) 737-2617

SOUTH DAKOTA Department of Labor, 700 Governor's Drive, Pierre, SD 57402-4730, (605) 733-3101

TENNESSEE Department of Employment Security, 500 James Robertson Parkway, 12th Floor-Volunteer Plaza, Nashville, TN 37245-0001, (615) 741-2131

TEXAS Workforce Commission, 101 E. 15th Street, Austin, TX 78778, (512) 463-2213

UTAH Department of Workforce Services, 140 East 300 South, P.O. Box 143001, Salt Lake City, UT 84114-3001, (801) 531-3780

VERMONT Department of Employment and Training, P.O. Box 488, Montpelier, VT 05601-0488, (802) 828-4300

VIRGIN ISLANDS Department of Labor, 2131 Hospital Street, Christianstead, St. Croix, USVI 00802, (809) 773-1994

VIRGINIA Employment Commission, 703 East Main Street, Richmond, VA 23219, (804) 786-3001

WASHINGTON Employment Security Department, P.O. Box 9046, Olympia, WA 98507-9046, (360) 902-9301

WEST VIRGINIA Bureau Employment Security, 112 California Avenue, Charleston, WV 25305-0112, (304) 558-2630

WISCONSIN Department of Industry, Labor & Human Relations, P.O. Box 7946, Madison, WI 53707, (608) 266-7552

WYOMING Department of Employment, 122 West 25th Street, Herschler Bldg., 2nd Floor, Cheyenne, WY 82002, (307) 777-6402

NATIONAL OFFICE UNITED STATES Employment Service, 200 Constitution Ave., NW, Room N-4470, Washington, DC 20210, (202) 219-219-5257

INDEX

Biography

Marc Sanders is a writer, mediator, trainer and musician. Co-author of the book, *The Lives and Times of Black Dallas Women* (Eakin Press 2002), Sanders teaches seminars in anger management, conflict resolution, negotiation, collaborative problem-solving and diversity. He holds a master's degree in organizational management. A former professional employment counselor, Marc writes résumés on a freelance basis. He resides in Austin, Texas.

0-595-26116-7